This deeply personal work is elevated by a voice both refreshing and unsettling in its directness as Aline Soules charts the unsentimental and courageous journey of her own heart . . . her poetry can startle with its sudden leaps between worlds, or its understatement, as in the haunting "Spilt Milk" . . . her surrender to each subject gives her voice its impressive range—from the lyrical recollections of first love to the wry humor of "Tea and Biscuits."

Mary Y. Hebert
Author of *Horatio Rides the Wind*
And contributing editor of *Not Black and White: Inside Words from the Bronx WritersCorps*

Aline Soules' personal world is larger than most—with poems and stories about places ranging from Rome to Scotland to Canada to Poland. She's best at recreating history, putting flesh on her childhood, her family, her son, the difficult and beautiful relationship with her parents and grandmother. In "The Size of the World," Aline Soules' voice is clear and serious, always leading us closer to those illusive concepts of truth, meaning, and compassion.

David James
Author of *A Heart out of This World*

With the eyes of a photographer and the writer's pen, Aline Soules walks the reader through the front door where we feel . . . her father's fingers sweep the strand of hair behind her ear, see him touch her mother's cheek, cup her chin, and look back one more time.

Mary Ann Wehler
Author of *Walking Through Deep Snow*

1

This is the first in a series of Plain View Press Flip-books, which combine the work of two writers whose art is closely linked and whose voices complement each other in terms of vision, content, and style.

To Bill:
I hope you enjoy
the book.
Aline
Mar 18, 2000

The Size of the World

Aline Soules

Plain View Press
P.O. 33311
Austin, TX 78764

Phone/Fax: 512-441-2452
e-mail: sbpvp@eden.com
http:www.eden.com/~sbpvp

ISBN: 1-891386-06-9
Library of Congress: 99-61023

Acknowledgements

The author wishes to acknowledge the following:

"Back Porch" in *A Century of Voices*, Detroit Women Writers, 1999 and *Variations on the Ordinary*, Plain View Press, 1995; "Let's Just Go On" in *Literature of the Expanding Frontier*, Prentice-Hall, 1999, "My Mama Always Said," *Verity Press*, 1998, *Heartsongs*, Poetry Society of Michigan, 1995 and *Variations on the Ordinary*, Plain View Press, 1995; "Wayburn Street" and "Lament for a Field" in *The MacGuffin*, 1998-1999; "From a Letter Dated 11 oct. 1916" (earlier version). "Dreamworld," "What We Remember," and "By Way of Vladivostok" (earlier version) in *100 Words*, 1996-1998; "In the Beginning" and "The Size of the World" in *Womankind*, 1996, Anderie Poetry Press, 1997; "Please" in *Prism III*; *Writing to Stop Violence Against Women*, University of Michigan, 1996; "Nothing" in *Mobius*, 1996; and "From Horizontal to Rest" in *Poet's Park* <http://www.soos.com/poetpark>, 1995. "Living Easy" first appeared in *Sistersong: Women Across Cultures*, 1998 and received Second Place in the 1996 Oakland University/Detroit Monthly Short Story Contest; "Dandelions and Blue Daisies" received Second Place in the 1996 Open Short Story Contest, North American International Auto Show and Honorable Mention in the 1995 Oakland University/Detroit Monthly Short Story Contest.

Cover art by Miriam Moore.

This book is dedicated to my mother
Harriet Flora Craig Stark Stannard
1908—1986
who showed me the size of the world.

Contents

In the Beginning

Granny wasn't like my friends' grandmothers, kind, sweet, or an endless source of cookies. She snapped and bit when she spoke, and said she didn't like children. She acted as if my dog didn't exist.

Even though she lived with us, I didn't see her during the day. Mysterious medical things happened in her room—I never knew what—but every evening, before I went to bed, I was ushered into her presence to say goodnight. Mother left me there while she prepared Granny's medicine.

Granny would bark questions and I would answer "Yes, Granny" or "No, Granny" or just nod. She often complained on Mother's return. "Flora, this child says she can read, but she can't knit." I learned to knit. "Flora, this child says she can do sums, but she's never embroidered." I learned to embroider.

One evening, as I came into the room, Granny had a brown leather case on her knees and was pulling on a pair of pink knit gloves with no fingers. I offered to knit her a new pair. "Nonsense, they're supposed to be like this." She held out her hands and sure enough, the gloves were knit with no fingers. "Keeps my hands warm while I write," she said.

She opened the case, took out a silver filigree container, unscrewed the cap and dipped in her pen. It was an inkwell. "My travel set," she said. "It suits me when I write in bed." She let me look inside. Deep blue india ink.

"What are you writing, Granny?" "None of your business," she said. "I don't ask what you write, do I?" "I don't write anything." Mother came into the room. "Flora, this child says she doesn't write anything."

The next night and from then on, Granny and I wrote, each in our own composition books because Granny didn't believe in diaries you bought. After all, you might not want to write the same amount every day.

"Why do we write?" I asked. "To know where we're going," she said. We never discussed it again. We just wrote. She wrote in hers until she couldn't write anymore. I still write in mine.

From a Letter dated 11 Oct. 1916, from John Nigel Stark to his daughter
Flora, age 8, 7e Region, Place de Villeneuve-S-Lot,
Hôpital de LaMothe, no. 115 bis

My darling Flora,

This is a lovely place with a river shining in the sunlight or—as I saw it last night—in the white moonlight.

All the cows which drag carts wear veils over their faces to protect them from flies and dust. At night, frogs make a great croaking noise and grasshoppers jump enormous distances. Lizards dart about the roads when the sun is strong or laze on sunny parts of the walls.

We have soldiers who were wounded at Verdun. One man is nearly well and will be back to war soon. I hope you are doing well in school and are careful when you are out by yourself.

Your Loving
Daddy

The Wren

Do you want to hold him
before we let him go?
asks Mother. I hold out my hands
for the bird that has flown
down the chimney
into our kitchen.

He is all heart. His beats
throb against
my cupped palms. I fear
his fear. Maybe he will die
right here in my hands.

Don't let him go in the house.
Mother senses I am about
to uncurl my fingers.
Let's take him outside.

We stand in the doorway.
Throw him up and out,
says Mother, *and he'll*
catch the wind.

Now, I don't want
to let him go. I will never have
this chance again—to hold
such wildness in my hands.
Go on, says Mother. *Now.*

I thrust my arms up
and out. He flutters off
balance, then finds an updraft.
I watch him fly and suddenly
know that it will be
my turn. Someday.

Dreamworld

My son draws a blue-green dream
on a piece of paper, a dream
of summer and sky.

We tape it to the window
and the sun shines through,
turning it translucent and warm.

We can leave this dreamworld flat
or take it from the window to scrumple
into an earth-shaped ball,

but when we reach for the dream,
we see the world again, this time
the one beyond the sunlit paper.

A tiny hornet, stinger not yet formed,
crawls behind the dream, as real in shadow
as the dream is in light.

On Seeing "Interior with Lady, Danish, 1905"

Detroit Institute of Arts

You sew in the light from the window.
Head bent, you do not see the silver sun
filter through lace curtains onto the floor
or send shadows of the window frame
onto the wood of the dining room table,

so perfectly polished. It's not your fault,
caught in your everyday world by the man
who painted you. It is only we
who can see the beauty of the light,
so distant in time and place, but even for us

it's not real, just a dream made of paint, and you,
dear lady, merely complete the background.
Tomorrow, when the dream is yesterday's
memory, will we see our own light, or will we,
like you, bend our heads to daily tasks
and fade into someone else's composition?

Beyond Reach

From my upper story window, I look
down on the morning park. It is covered
with a blanket of fog and the tops
of the dandelion puffs break the surface,
white on light grey. Across the park

are houses like mine in mirror image,
but I will have to walk on water
to reach my reflection in their windows.
Later, the sun will steam the blanket away
as if it had never been, and I will see

the puffs like coarse salt on the green.
Children will grind them beneath their heels
or kick them in the air like wisps of fog
the sun forgot, and I will walk across
their broken stems without a thought.

Back Porch

A back porch is honest.
Old rambling roses
you planted when you moved in
crawl untended up its poles
and trail over the roof.
The wooden planks are cracked
and the flaking paint is splotched
with green and red
from your children's paintbox.

Slouched in an old chair
no longer good enough
for the living room,
you don't worry about
offending sensibilities
with old work clothes or dirty boots.
You relax with a cup of tea,
leave a wet ring on the sloping floor
and smell the roses with the chicken
roasting for dinner in the kitchen beyond.

Leaning back, you think
about nothing and everything—
when your son is due back
from hockey, the light
through the rose petals, the diet
you'll never start, the last time
you made love.

As the sun slants deeper,
shadows lengthen across the floor
and mingle against the sides
of the house—roses, the chair,
the poles that connect
the railings to the roof,
and you.

If Only

If only I could be with you on Loch Fyne, the morning water a black china plate, still except for the ripples from your dipped oars. If only I could share your rhythm as you row down the loch with the tide. Loose seaweed, we would float in the wake and I would remember . . .

O

At eight years of age, we fight over the dead fish we have spent the day catching with boom, lead and line. Our knives flash in the sun as the blades slit the fish from anus to head. The sun warms our backs as we clean the fish in sea water, entrails taken away by the tide. Our sweat builds as we work fast, heads bent to the task, not seeing the sun, the water, ourselves. We are fish, knife, entrails, sweat and smell.

O

The night is black with no moon. Perfect for poaching fish. I go out with you and your father, the two of you pulling oars together, me in the stern, facing the bow and the wind, and watching your faces as you pull the boat through the water. I am grown now. It has been a long time since I went away, but now that I am back, I feel as if I still belong. I am warm in your heavy coat, but the wind is cold on my face, and my fingers are icy from trailing them in the water to see the sparkle of phosphorescence that always amazes me. Your father sets dynamite at the mouth of the river and I can feel the strength of your muscles as you take both oars and pull us away from the muffled blast as fast as you can. We wait to make sure no one has heard, but the black night is not disturbed, and we go back with nets to pull all the fish that have been foolish enough to try to swim up river to spawn.

O

Teenagers, we row the boat across the loch to the cave, stroking even, so the boat will go straight. Our rhythm takes us past the island, through its shadow and out the other side. As we near the cave, we pull hard to gain the speed to scrape through the opening that is just wide enough for the boat to pass. As we reach it, we slip the oars from the rowlocks and drop them and ourselves to the bottom of the boat. The water we shipped on our way across is cold on our backs, the cave cool after the sun and the effort. We make no attempt to rise.

O

It is your parents' turn to have the spring gathering. Some of the men are at the shore, mending boats; others are in the fields, planting oats. The women are in the kitchen, preparing for mid-day dinner. The older children must work with the men and women, but we smaller ones are free for the day. We play Rob Roy MacGregor, Treasure Island. We roam the fields, the steading, the byre, the house, the shore. We are shooed away when we come too close to the work. In mid-afternoon, you and I find the perfect spot to escape the terrible English. We steal jeelie pieces from the plate for tea and climb up the drain pipe to the roof of the house. It is warm and we understand why the sheep like to lie in the middle of the road. We look down on the pattern below—men, tractors, children, boats, water, more children, everything moving across the still earth. We hear the women's voices through the open windows of the kitchen—some English, some Gaelic, laughter, teasing. Later, after we sneak back down, we tell no one where we've been. It is our secret and we just know that this is the way it is.

O

We are in the upper field, stooking wheat that your older brothers have cut down and tied into bundles. We make each stook by balancing one sheaf against another, three pairs across, one on each end. It threatens to rain, so we pile them up as fast as we can.

17

The dogs are lying by the haystacks, watching your brothers building another stack. One is on top, laying sheaves around the circle. The other passes them up. As we near the end of the field, we start to feel the rain, slowly at first, then harder. You take a sheaf off the end of a stook and wriggle in backwards, grinning at me as I get wet. I quickly do the same and we stare at each other from our separate wheat tents across the wet expanse of stubble. When the storm is over, we crawl out and, with the others, pile on the tractor and in the jeep to go home. Suddenly we realize that Belle is not with the other dogs. Ready to have her litter, she has crawled under a haystack. We must coax her out and pull the pups after, keeping them in her sight so she doesn't panic. I sit in the back of the jeep, your coat across my knees, nine pups crawling on top. Belle stands on the floor as best she can, nuzzling her pups and licking them as we bump across the field and down the road to your house.

○

It is high summer and your family is going to Dunoon for the games. You all pile into two cars and disappear down the road. I am left standing in the farmyard. I came because I wanted to go, but this is a family outing and I am not invited. I watch the two cars top the hill and drive out of sight. I turn my back and walk along the edge of the road that is also a seawall. My vision is so blurred with tears that I slip and fall to the rocks and pebbles below. It is only three feet, but my legs are scraped. I run home with bleeding legs and bruised pride.

○

I have been gone a long time—nine years, but I feel the same about you as when I was fifteen, and I hope you do, too. It is Saturday night and we go to town for the dance. We can either go to the Scottish fling, which your parents urge us to do because they think I must "be missing the reels," or we can go with the others to the hall with its loud band and strong beat. We go to the hall. The lights are down and we take to the floor. You want to introduce me to your friends, but I just want you. In the end, I am too obvious.

You have little choice and you dance with me alone. We start to kiss in the dark, caught up in the beat of the music and ourselves. At the end of the night, the air outside the hall feels cool against our hot bodies. On the way home, we kiss in the back of the car as your brother and sisters drive home in silence. I cling to you when we get out of the car, but in my heart I know our time has passed. It is too late for us.

○

I wish I could see the seals, basking on the island, splayed on top of each other, the color of the rocks. I can grab seaweed in my hand, scoop it up and let the water run through my fingers. I can pop its bubbles, but I cannot touch you, not even in my mind. The seals melt into the dark gray background, lost in the shadow of the island, then slip into the water and disappear.

What We Remember

The thread from the hem of my jacket remembers
the shape of its stitches even as I toss it away,
but I remember the days when my mother and I
would pick out the stitches from the french cuffs
on my father's shirts or unravel two sweaters
I had outgrown, washing the threads to make them forget
before we reversed the cuffs to sew them back on
or knitted a new striped sweater from the two skeins.

The Hills and the Sea and the River

I am six and I have been sent to my room for some fault I no longer remember. I lie on the bed, anger a lump in my throat, tears blurring my eyes. *I hate you, I hate you*, I think, as I lie in the gloaming, waiting for the long day to end. I do not see out the window, where the sun sets over the hills and the sea pours in to fill the wide mud flats of the river.

○

I am ten and I do not want to go. I do not want to leave this house. Mother and I stand in the street and watch bailiffs throw out our furniture. They nail boards across the windows and doors of what we once called home. We turn our backs and walk to town, leaving everything sitting in the rain as the twilight turns to night.

○

I am seventeen. I stand by another river half a world away. There are no hills in Detroit and the river isn't even a river. It's a strait. In winter, ice flows in chunks, swift with the current and cold like this place where I live.

○

I am thirty-five and I have brought my son to this river that isn't a river. It is an early Spring day that makes us want to jump and shout. So we do. We run, and we throw stones and sticks on the water and watch them float away fast, but it is a long way to the sea. They are heading in the direction of my hills and my sea and my river, but most will snag on a rock or drift ashore in some new place.

○

I am forty-seven and I sit in the Invercarse Hotel with my friend Christine. We are silent, even though we have not seen one another for six years. Before us are the hills and the sea and the river. There is nothing we need to say.

Playing Hooky

Do it again! Faster! shout the boys
from the back seat of the car as we
bump over railroad tracks and they
rise to the occasion. I turn and go back
again and again, until they're ready to quit.
A policeman stares from his parked car,
but smiles when I catch his eye.

A day of sun and warmth in mid-October.
I have left unmade beds and dirty dishes.
The garden needs spading. The roses
are free to grow without pruning. We run
in the woods, crunch apples at the orchard,
eat three of the four food groups in cider,
doughnuts and ice cream.

The horse in the field past the orchard
hangs back. Andy leans over the fence
to beckon, but jumps at the electric ripple
up his arm. *Race you,* he yells as he takes off
for the end of the lane, Craig right behind.
They run out of steam half way to the road
and kick stones along the tractor ruts.

The sun is low. The translucent gold it gave
to the leaves fades. As I turn east to drive home
along Waltz Road, I glance in the rear view mirror.
The sun glints off the boys' hair as they fall
asleep. I want to watch them forever, but
I must turn back to the road. I am alone
with this fleeting and unrepeatable day.

What If

What if you had held me
when I was an infant, cooed at me
and told me stories?

Or said *God made it that way*
when I asked why
the sky was blue?

What if you had written to me
when you had your nervous breakdown
and left?

Or told me you loved me when you came
back through the door, instead of pretending
it had never happened?

Mother said you were afraid I would fall
from your arms, that you didn't
hold me until I was six months old.

You explained the laws of physics
over and over,
but I couldn't follow you.

You disappeared
from my life
like a mirage.

Yet now, my mind sees this image:
you're Charlie Chaplin
tied to a track, waiting

for a train to roll over you
so you can save me
from the truth.

Rag Dolls

Lulu, Mimi and Fifi
God how I loved them
arms and legs splayed
bodies gray and dingy
necks clutched
thinner
thinner
heads angled
steeper
steeper
just like my mother
the day she died.

Waking You in Early Morning

I wake you to see the rainbow,
a perfect semicircle across a dark sky.
You can hardly open your eyes.

If this were my rainbow, we
would make love now, but you
are too tired and I must go to work.

Tonight, you will want me to see
the clear moon, but
it will be my turn to be tired

so I will go to bed and you
will read late, falling asleep
in the chair downstairs.

Tomorrow, there will be no rainbow,
and the moon will turn yellow
behind a cloud.

Gas Comes to Town

Neighbor women huddle in the corner
as far from the new gas stove
as they can get. *Oh, Flora, it'll blow up,*
cries one woman as Mother lights
a long match.

Gas comes to our house.
It's a bumper year. Gas, electricity
and running water. Overnight,
we pop from one era to another.

Daily, my father crosses time
from our nineteenth-century house to
his twentieth-century office. Soon,
he brings home every gadget
he can afford—the magic of a washer
and dryer, the world of TV.

But gas comes first, so the stove
is number one—small, two burners,
with a little oven and a slot called a broiler
inbetween. Before the collective gasp
is over, Mother wields the long match
like D'Artagnan, and lights all three.
Rows of blue flames appear, but no
explosion. *It's a miracle*, says one.

The women make toast—scads of it.
They put the bread on the broiler tray
and toast one side until it curls up
toward the flame. They turn it over
with a fork to toast the other side
until it flattens out again.

And then, holy of holies, they put butter
on the toast, a week's worth of rations plus
a precious hoard one woman
brought from her sister's farm.

We children, only allowed
to peer through the kitchen window,
demand to get in. We bang
on the window and rush
to the door, jumping up
and down. At last, they open it
and we tumble into our new world.

History Lessons

We were taught English history in my Scottish primary school, but I didn't know it for a long time. The teaching of English history must have started after England conquered the last of Scotland in 1745, but to us, history was just what we were told in the form of facts and dates that we memorized. By my fourth year in school, we had covered key events up to the great Elizabeth I—Arthur and the burning of the cakes, King Canute's inability to turn back the tide, the Norman Conquest, the Plantagenets, the Wars of the Roses, and the Tudors, including Henry VIII and his six wives.

In Primary Four, we started on Elizabeth I, including her ploys and battles with Mary Queen of Scots that resulted in Mary's beheading. After that, Mary's son James came in line for the throne and we were told that James VI of Scotland became James I of England. My mind, having now been trained in arithmetic, wondered what had happened to James I through V, so one day, I raised my hand and asked. Not a good idea. I was told to sit down in a tone of voice I didn't want to cross. I sat down.

I said nothing to my mother about this event because I thought I'd just get into more trouble, so the question went unanswered for the rest of the year. James VI travelled down to England and we learned about the English court of that and later days, although not about the relationships courtiers had with their royal masters, a topic I didn't know enough to question at all. History marched on through the centuries, the rest of that school year and the next.

In Primary Six, I had Mr. Sanderson. He believed in history as whole cloth, so he'd pick a date, put it on the blackboard and run back and forth along its length, writing down events around the world. He might choose 1848 and then write what was happening in England, France, Prussia, the United States and China. His other game was to come to class dressed as a character from the period we were studying. Our job was to guess who he was. To be ready for class, however, he had to walk the halls in these costumes (male, female, current, ancient). As a result, he was viewed as the school eccentric and some of the parents and teachers weren't too happy.

Our theory was that he scared our old fogey parents and made the other teachers jealous.

Towards the end of the year, when we'd finished what we had to learn (we were preparing to write our "Eleven Plus" exams the following year), Mr. Sanderson came into class one day and said "Ask me anything." At first there was silence, but that niggling question had quickly come into my mind and, in spite of my slightly churning stomach, I took the chance. "What happened to James 1 through V?" I asked. Mr. Sanderson gave me a long look, then he began to answer. For the rest of the term, he told us our story—Wallace and Bruce, Malcolm Canmore and St. Margaret, the Stuarts, the Border wars, Katherine Barlass.

I never heard about these people again in my formal schooling. I didn't hear about them at all in Primary Seven and I never asked. Then I moved to Canada. In my first year in high school, we studied British history, but I knew better—it was English history taught from a book with a Beefeater on the front cover. Canadians were still part of the British Commonwealth and Ontario, where I was living, was often more English than England.

Over the next couple of years, we studied ancient and modern world history from a western perspective. Already skeptical, I took much of this with a grain of salt, but in my final year, lesson number one was reinforced and I got lesson number two. We studied the history of America, meaning the United States and Canada. For Canadians, the United States was not America—it was the United States. America meant North America and included both the United States and Canada. Unfortunately for the teacher, our class had a young man of Mexican descent. How he'd ended up in Windsor, Ontario, was a mystery, but there he was. He started to argue that America meant his country, too, and Brazil and Argentina and all the rest of South America, and he kept it up all year, interrupting every time the term America was used in the narrow sense of North America. If we hadn't had central exams that were marked in Toronto, I expect he would have flunked. As it was, his marks weren't too good through the year, but he aced the exam and passed with a high enough grade to go on to college without a problem.

While he was arguing off and on about the definition of America, we were studying such topics as the "United States" Revolution, the War of 1812 and the "United States" Civil War. The study of war is fascinating—not the boring battles or the dates one later forgets, but the way it is taught. When the U.S. Revolution had come up in my Scottish primary school, we spent barely half a lesson on it. A colony rebelled against England and was no longer part of the picture. When I took this subject in Canada, we spent about two weeks on it, much of it in comparison to Canada's own upcoming struggle to establish a less subservient role to the "United Kingdom."

What we really spent time on was the War of 1812. While interesting events happened locally with Commander Perry and Lake Erie, the real key to this emphasis was the fact that Canada won, even though it was still British North America. The United States was drawn into the discussion, but my main recollection was learning that its national anthem was based on a battle in Baltimore. The U.S. Civil War was covered in about the same amount of time as its Revolution and was not presented any differently from any other war. African Americans, as they are currently known, were mere instruments in the fight for their rights, northern white men taking the noble roles. Native Americans were briefly mentioned later in U.S. chronology when white men conquered the west and as for women, they appeared only occasionally in support roles. The only time they took any place of their own was during the period of the suffragettes, who were treated as comical figures.

In 1971, I moved to the United States and about a year later, I began a degree in library science. Although I wasn't taking history, I did get some more lessons. An argument broke out one day in the student lounge. One student insisted the national anthem was based on a battle from what she described as the "American" Civil War. The other student thought it came from the Spanish-American War. As a new immigrant, I had the pleasure of pointing out that it came from the War of 1812, a war that some of them didn't remember, assuming they had heard of it at all.

Some time after that, we got a Civil War buff in our program, one of those people who know every battle from the ground up. I admire people who can remember the kind of details he knew—numbers on each side, slope of the terrain (he'd visited most of the Civil War sites), details of clothing, nuances buried in original letters. He was truly wonderful and what I learned from him was the continuing and prevailing angst of a war that to this day is not resolved, a war that to many is the most important war this country has ever seen. As for the story of African Americans, Native Americans or women, their history is only now beginning to emerge in independent stories.

I have had the privilege of travelling in a number of countries and living extensively in three—Scotland, Canada and the United States. In each of these, the focus has been the same. Study your own history, study everyone else's from your own point of view, focus on the wars you won, downplay the ones you didn't and never teach anyone about their own history if you've conquered them.

Not long ago, I read in the paper that German children were woefully ignorant about the history of World War II. People were shocked, but I wasn't at all surprised.

By Way of Vladivostok

When World War I broke out, my grandfather left Poland and rode off to war on a horse. Before long, he was captured by the Russians and sent to the eastern end of Siberia. In the middle of winter, he escaped and, without proper food or clothing, headed south. His goal was to reach Vladivostok in order to find a ship and escape.

I don't know how long it took him to get there, but he did. He tried to find a ship's captain who would take him away, but he had no money and there were those he dared not ask. His attempts to stowaway were thwarted. After several weeks, he decided that he wasn't going to be able to escape by sea, so he turned his face west and started walking.

Vladivostok is on the very southeast tip of what was then becoming the Union of Soviet Socialist Republics. Due west is China, Mongolia, then Russia again, so he chose another route. He travelled southwest through China, across the top of Burma, across India, then through the Near East and Turkey. He found a way across the Bosporus, then headed north to Poland.

By the time he reached home, the war was almost over, tanks had replaced horses, and everyone thought he was dead. But he wasn't. He just knocked on the door, went in and took up his life. It wasn't World War I that got him. It was World War II when the Germans bombed Warsaw in the first week.

Let's Just Go On

When we emigrated to Ontario
from Scotland, I was a teenager.
We miss the hills and the sea, said Mother,

laying the groundwork for our first
and future summer vacations.
Mother and I went while Father worked.

She drove and I read the maps.
We camped to save money, but ate in restaurants
as she had to do all the driving.

The first summer, she told my father
we were going to the Smoky Mountains
in Tennessee. We slept by a bear trap.

A day or so later, she looked at the maps.
It's not that far to the sea, she said,
Let's just go on. We sent postcards from Florida.

The next year, she told my father
we were going to the Black Hills
in South Dakota. We lost our tarp to hailstones.

A day or so later, she looked at the maps.
It's not that far to the sea, she said,
Let's just go on. We sent postcards from San Francisco.

We saw forty-eight states and ten provinces
in five years. I got to be the best map reader around,
and Father stopped asking where we were going.

Spilt Milk

Milk drips off the kitchen table
on to the broken glass from the bottle
shattered across the floor, but no one
is in the kitchen any more. Mother
and I are in the downstairs hall,
holding hands. You, Father, stride
through every room in the house.

First, you are in the garage. Now,
you hold hands with an axe. You go
upstairs to the bedroom you share
with Mother. Wood splinters with
startled cracks. Floorboards creak
above my head as you cross
the hall to my room. Glass

is a waterfall as it skitters across
oak boards, splinters off the hand
rail and clink, clink, clinks down
the stairs. A green shard from the vase
you gave me for my birthday lands
at my feet. I wonder if my dolly
is all right. You come back

downstairs. You are in the dining room.
I see the oak table through the doorway,
watch each leg break and fall under
your strength. As you pass us on your
way to the living room, you reach out
to sweep a strand of hair behind my ear.
I cling harder to Mother's hand.

When you are done, you drop the axe
at Mother's feet. You touch her cheek,
cup my chin in your hand. Mother and I
still hold hands as we watch you open
the front door and look back at us one
more time. The splinters fade into silence
as the latch clicks behind you.

Please

Don't mix my carrots with my peas,
please. I don't even want them
touching each other. And please
don't put my potatoes next to my meat.
The blood runs into the white smush
and turns it soggy and brown.

The water's too hot in the tub. I don't
care if I'm not squeaky clean. Please
don't make me get in. I don't want
that awful soap in my hair. It stings
my eyes. And don't cut my toenails
too close. The ends of my toes hurt.

Why do I have to go to bed now anyway?
I don't want to go to bed. I don't
want you next to me. Please,
Daddy. Your breath is hot and your hands
hurt and you're heavy when you lie
on top of me. Besides, I don't like
the way the sun turns brown
through the curtains and makes
shadows on the white wall.

Nothing

When we write with a pen
or read a book, the word
is what we see. The space
is nothing. It is just before
and after, to keep the words
apart. But, in computers,
that nothing is something,
as real as a letter or number,
equal in its own place.

Likewise, there is a time
to sow and a time to reap,
but there is also a time inbetween, a time to do
nothing, to let the mind
drift. In looking back,
shouldn't we remember
more than the words
of our lives—the births,
the deaths, the letters,
the numbers? Shouldn't we
also think back to the time
we were fallow, growing
in silence and space?

Jogging

With loping stride,
my son starts his daily jog
down the sidewalks
of our neighborhood.

Long and lean,
he moves with easy grace,
so different from the jerky
toddler who chased a ball
too close to the street.

He is no longer the boy
who kicked stones from his path
on the way to school,
the taut-muscled kid
who rushed to play with his friends,
the stumbling youth on a walk
with his first girlfriend.

I watch him grow
smaller in the distance,
turn the corner
and disappear.

The Pane

from the photograph of a young girl
looking out a window

Girl in a white dress, locked in your lace,
what do you see through the window
beyond the sunlight and the trees?

Flatten your nose on the hard pane. Press
out. Even though you cloud it with your breath
until you cannot see through the glass, in time
you will open the window to the fullness
of leaves and the heat of the shining sun.

Then you will begin to see beyond,
to what you could not see before. Press
on. Do not look back. Do not seek
refuge in the shade of the room
you chose to leave behind.

The Size of the World

As a small child, my mother lay in the long Scottish night dreaming of places worlds away—Rio, San Francisco, Zanzibar.

Now, she lies on a hospital bed, her limbs like sticks, her shanks encased in a diaper which she plucks with her fingers. "I don't want this," she whispers, but it is too much to expect nurses to clean her when there are so many to tend.

Her name is Harriet Flora Craig Stark Stannard—so much for such a little person. She no longer answers to Mrs. Stannard or Mother, or to the nurses when they call her Harriet, for she has always gone by Flora. I explain this when I can, but there is always someone new who doesn't understand and writes on her chart: No Response.

Even I must call her Flora, as if she were my child. Then she stares at me with blue bright eyes. I remember to put on her glasses, but most of the time, they lie in the drawer by the side of the bed. Without them, she sees only shapes.

One day, she asks for her coat. "It's time to go," she says. I say nothing. A day later she asks again, "Where's my coat?" I promise to bring it.

On my next visit, I walk past the nurses' station with her winter coat over my arm. They follow me with their eyes as I pass. When I enter the room and put on her glasses, Mother sees the coat. She lifts the covers with a trembling hand until she can raise her leg. Both hang in the air as she tries to gather strength.

I do not help her. I do not speak. She lowers her leg and the covers. I hang the coat in the empty closet. "When you're ready, it'll be here," I say. She never mentions it again.

As the days pass, I move closer to her body when I talk to her. I stroke her hand and brush her hair. I sing, just for her. This woman, who traveled to all the places of her childhood dreams, now lives in a world smaller than a baby's crib.

The Swing

After World War II, many men of Polish background, including my father, ended up in Scotland, married to Scottish women. He used to play poker with Polish friends who had the same experience. I couldn't pronounce their names, so I called them One-o-vitch, Two-o-vitch, Three-o-vitch and Four-o-vitch. I was particularly fond of Three-o-vitch who never came to visit without a treat. At night, when I was supposed to be in bed, I would often crawl out and lie on the cold floor of my bedroom with my ear to the corner above the dining room where they played. They regaled each other with humorous episodes from the war. No matter what the hidden horror, there was only laughter and a camaraderie that could never have developed in peace time.

One Christmas, my father talked a couple of them into helping him put up a swing for me in the back yard. This event took place during the night of December 24 after I was in bed. Santa was supposed to be the bringer of this great gift. They started by digging two large holes in which to place concrete blocks to anchor the swing. The work was heavy and cold. They periodically took breaks in the garage where they took a wee nip from a bottle of whisky. By the middle of the night, they might or might not have been warm, but they were past caring. The noise rose and songs broke out, then my father decided they should take a dram for every comrade who had died at Arnhem. As his platoon of thirty-eight men had been dropped by parachute and he had come back with only three, this was quite an undertaking. Wakened by the commotion, I watched from my bedroom window until I heard my mother tell them to "shush." I slipped back in bed when she came upstairs to see if I was still asleep.

In the morning, I looked out the window to see Three-o-vitch slumped against the metal post of the swing, his head on his chest. The others were nowhere to be seen. On rushing downstairs, my mother told me to be quiet as my father was still in bed. I knew better than to ask about the others, as I was not supposed to know they had been there in the first place. Besides, I wanted that swing. By the time I was taken outside, Three-o-vitch had gone, but so had Santa. He was as gone as the goose we ate for dinner, and it took me until I had my own child before I found him again. 41

Taking Down Your Tree House

for my son

The clatter of broken boards echoes
thunder moving in from the west.
We take down your tree house as fast as we can,
hoping to beat the storm. We balance
on either end of the floor so we don't fall.

Nails fly in all directions as you wrench them
from the wood with a claw hammer. You rip
open the roof and expose us
to the ominous sky, take down walls,
widen windows until they disappear.

Your back curves, your muscles flex,
your legs brace against shuddering tree limbs.
All I can do in the hot, thick air is take boards
from your hands and drop one
on top of the other in a pile below.

I wanted to take down the tree house last year.
You didn't use it all summer, and I thought
it was time, but you begged me to leave it.
At night, you wouldn't sleep for fear
I would take it down while you dreamed.

Now, you are one smooth motion after another,
caught in the rhythm as you tear it apart
without a thought. Tonight, you will fall
into dreamless sleep, as if it had never been,
while I listen to rain against the broken boards.

Lament for a Field

Tassels dapple the green with gold. In a fallow year,
the field grows chicory, Queen Anne's lace, wild statice.
Once, it was full of gray-green cabbages, round
and dense with strong leaves. They grew with the season.
One day, they were gone. This year, it is cabbages again,
as full as before, but almost hidden in the brush
at the edge of the field is a sign: For Sale, 80 acres.

The field lies brown through fall and early winter, until snow
dots it like powder, then falls in a solid cloak. In spring,
it turns from gray to brown, speckled with gulls that feed
on a crop of worms raised by a tractor that shapes the field
into furrows, throws herringbone clods of earth into air.
At day's end, the farmer leaves footprints in the field,
but the field follows him home, clinging to his feet like an echo.

Rain leaves lakes in the furrows and tractor ruts. Weeping willows
trail fronds in the puddles. The field holds leaves, sky, and clouds
in its watery folds, even a plane that skims the surface,
then seeps into wet earth. It grows so full, it oozes into the roots
of the willows, cries into ditches, and weeps into the creek
at the end of the road. The farmer waits, unable to walk
the sodden ground. The field waits for a season that will not come.

Surrender

I'm glad my father is dead.
He would have hated this fiftieth
anniversary of World War II, men
in their eighties parading across
now-sunny, grassy fields of St. Lo,
wearing Black Watch tartan or
old army uniforms, their medals,
reminiscing on TV about
the best times in their lives.

He would not have wanted
to remember the raw and rotten
turnips he stole from half-frozen
fields at night, sneaking out
from dark woods where Russians
chased him night and day for six weeks,
unrelenting until winter turned to spring
and they had to return to the front.

He wanted to forget his escape
from Russia and the two thousand mile
trek across Europe, through Hungary,
Yugoslavia, Italy, France, all with
a bullet in his leg, but the bullet
wouldn't let him. All his life,
it threw clots that travelled the miles
of his arteries to punish him with pain.

He hid in a drawer the Croix de Guerre
he was given near the end of the war
when he captured a unit of Germans
by himself. Lost, he pretended to be
a scout and conned them into thinking
he had the whole army behind him.
They couldn't wait to surrender
and, in the end, neither could he.

My Family at Home

I only lived in Rome once, when I was about four. Father spoke Italian fluently, but Mother waved her arms a lot. She fit right in. Our landlady wore black bombazine and had to turn sideways to fit through the door. She took me to the market where people shouted and vegetables came in purple and red and yellow. They weren't like the gray granite shops of our home in Scotland where everything was pale and wrinkled and Mr. MacLeish told me not to touch anything. It didn't matter much because next year, we were in Eindhoven and the year after that, in Nantes, where we lived in a round tower with a spiral staircase in the middle, and all the rooms were shaped like slices of pie with a bite taken out.

It was my aunt who stayed in one place, once she got there—Kenya—although there was the time she spent in Assam where it was so damp that every morning, she had to scrape the green mold out of her shoes. Then there were my cousins. They grew up in Africa, when they weren't shipped home because of the war or boarding school. Nigel went back to work on the Serengeti Plain, but Fiona married someone from Yorkshire and moved to New York. Then she lived in Florida. That's where they all end up, if they come from New York.

Then there are my other cousins. The one born in Toronto was taken to Houston when she was a toddler. That's where her sister was born. Then they moved to London where they got a layer of Cockney over their Texas drawl. No one could understand them for months. Of course, they grew up too. Jane ended up in Dubai for a while, then Mill Valley, California. Alison tried Swansea and finally married and moved to France.

As for me, I'm on my third country now, but that's the way my family is. There are other, more distant cousins in Hong Kong and New Zealand and Mauritius. There's only one thing—no one lives in Scotland any more.

Tea and Biscuits

Escape from school on a weekday morning. We wait on the railway platform for my bedridden Granny to arrive by train. Everything is ready—a gurney to carry her up the steps of the station, an ambulance to bring her to the house, two attendants, and a taxi to drive Mother and me home behind the ambulance. The train is due at 9:57—one of those strange times only used by the British railway system. It arrives on time.

I can hear Granny's voice from inside the train. She wants her blanket re-arranged, not the green one, the blue one, which shouldn't touch the sides of the train or trail on the floor. Her head hurts and the attendant is pulling her shoulder. He should be more careful. The attendants carry on and her voice rises.

The journey from Edinburgh to Dundee is only an hour, but it's too long and too far—a lifetime. She has left her home forever to come to the last place she will live in her life—and she knows it. It takes another hour to maneuver her off the train, transfer her from the narrow litter to the gurney, carry her up the steps, and place her in the ambulance.

The ambulance looks much the same as the police vans that scoop up drunks on Friday night at closing time. It's black with no windows in the back, so Granny disappears into deep gloom. The taxi is black, too—one of those tall Victorian cabs now only seen in old movies. We climb into the cab and the procession begins.

The Dundee train station is by the river. To get to the High Street, we must ride up Whitehall, which is steep and rough with cobblestones. The ambulance lurches up the road and signals, but as it turns, the wheel falls off the back left and bounds down the road, leaping past my face as I look out the taxi window. The ambulance teeters on the cusp of the road, then settles at an angle on its empty axle.

Everyone stops and rushes to the back of the ambulance. The driver flings open the doors.

"Are you all right, Mrs. Stark?" he calls into the black interior.

"I want tea and biscuits, and I want them NOW!" says Granny.

Mother sends me to Mr. Allen, the grocer. I run along the High Street, cross the road, and race up Reform Street.

"My Granny wants tea and biscuits, and she wants them now," I tell Mr. Allen, who is up a ladder sorting shelves. He looks at my face and tells me to follow. I have never been in the back of the shop, which is full of boxes and has a tiny stove, a long counter, a sink as big as our laundry tubs at home, and enormous burlap bags full of flour and beans and coffee and tea. I would like to explore, but I sense it is a privilege to be allowed in the back, so I stand still and watch while Mr. Allen sets the kettle to boil and empties his thermos for fresh tea.

"Does your granny take milk and sugar?" he asks.

I nod and he stirs them in. He fills a bag with the thermos and a one pound box of rich tea biscuits.

"Away off now," he says, so I thank him and run back.

The scene I left has grown. In addition to the ambulance and taxi, there are now one police car, two policemen, and a gathering crowd of women diverted from their weekly shopping. I give Mother the tea and biscuits, and the attendant hands them into the back of the ambulance. I hear the thermos being unscrewed, then the methodical crunch of biscuits.

It takes another hour for a new ambulance to arrive. As Granny is moved from one to the other, I see her lying flat, the thermos in the crook of her right arm and the box of biscuits in her left. Her eyes are closed and she says nothing. I wonder if she is falling asleep, but just as she is being lifted into the second ambulance, she opens her eyes and looks at me.

"I suppose you want one," she says to me.

I nod.

"Well, I ate them all," she says and closes her eyes again.

The procession makes its slow way home. Only when she is safely in her new bed does she let Mother take the thermos and the empty box from her grasp.

"Can't have the child growing up greedy," she says.

Taking the Plunge

Forehead on the glass elevator, pressing
as hard as I can, eyes fore-
shadowing what is to come, I feel
the hum of the engine, the release of
the cab and my stomach lurch
in that moment of
time.

This is what it is like to plunge off
a building, to free
fall down a shaft of gravity. What
would I think in these final minutes
if the world rose to meet me
for the last
time?

I would think of my father as he
calls out to me to live according to
his plan, makes me feel
small, even as he grows
smaller because I am
watching him
plunge for me
all the way
down.

Burial

At my father's grave, my mother's hand
shook on her four-footed cane as the minister
intoned words that neither of us heard.
We stared at the gravestone with his name
and hers, his birth year and hers,
carved into place by an unknown hand.

My father had wanted this double stone
to link him to my mother, even after death.
How could he have known the manner
of its making? How my mother
would find herself standing before
the beginning of her own end?

Which came soon enough. By then,
his death date was in place, but winter
kept the mason from carving hers.
The stone stood unfinished for months,
making my mother seem alive.

Only the raw earth gave any clue
that her body lay below.
That spring, as the sun grew warm enough
to be real, the mason returned.
The next time I visited was my last.

Wayburn Street

Tattered kids play with frayed ropes and leftover tin cans,
inventing a game on the broken concrete of the sidewalk.
No one plays in the street as they would in my neighborhood.
I drive right down the middle as if I were alone in the desert.

The street is lined with the charred shells of burned-out houses,
toothless gaps among the row of clapboard and broken brick.
Peeling gingerbread clings to the eaves. Plywood criss-crosses
windows. Porches list under the tired weight of old posts.

Mile-high weeds and open patches of chicory encroach on
the burned hulls. It reminds me of a childhood visit
to London, craters and rubble buried under fireweed
still there ten years after the blitz of World War II.

The spring sunshine is as out of place in this street as I am.
It catches the torn red shirt of a girl who hops, skips and
jumps, using the broken concrete patches as her squares.
Two teen boys swagger by, laughing and mimicking her.

The girl stops and stares after them as they jive to the rap
from the boom box one of them sports on his shoulder.
They see my car. I try not to look at them even as I feel
their eyes bore into my back. I check that my doors are

still locked, feeling ashamed as I do it. I can be no more
than eight or ten feet away from them, but here in this
alien place, this broken and beaten street, we are a world
and a lifetime apart. Never have I felt so white.

Dandelions and Blue Daisies

Laine didn't remember much about the house that burned down next door. There was a roar that woke her in the night. Then Ma bundled her in a blanket and took her outside to heat and red-yellow light, shouting people, thick arcs of water, but she didn't remember the house at all. Now it was just a black shell. Even sunshine couldn't reach inside. Ma complained about the weeds around it, but Laine thought they were flowers. She liked the yellows and the blues.

"The yellow ones is just dandelions, girl," Ma told her. "I don't know what the blue ones is. No, they're not daisies. They're not even flowers."

"Why?"

"They just grow. Real flowers you got to work at, like roses and things. Those things just come up anywhere."

Laine didn't get it. Sometimes, when she woke in the night, she saw them in the streetlight. They still looked good to her, even when their colors were weird. Sometimes, she woke at night to voices and saw boys trample them when they climbed into the black shell. The boys would disappear into it without a sound, as if they were never coming back, but in the morning they were gone and the dandelions and blue daisies would be upright again. After a while, she started talking to the flowers, telling them about school or asking them what to do when she didn't like one of Ma's boyfriends.

It wasn't that Laine didn't have a real friend. She did. Her name was Crystal and they were together a lot, but she and Crystal went to school together and Laine didn't want to talk about Ma's boyfriends. With Crystal, she wanted to forget all that. They talked about other stuff—clothes they'd buy if they ever got money, houses with nice furniture, and real yards with real flowers. Of course, Crystal thought like Ma. She liked roses and laughed at Laine when Laine said she was going to have dandelions and blue daisies, if she could ever figure out what they were.

Laine felt sorry for them because nobody wanted them. Besides, nobody else had any flowers. They had some coarse grass maybe, but mostly it was just broken toys or metal bits from cars no one had around anymore. Ma got rid of that stuff from their yard, but she wouldn't have flowers. "Too much work," she said.

Ma's boyfriends weren't much on that stuff either. One after another, they came and stayed for a while, then left. They liked to watch TV and drink beer. Some of them were okay, but most of them scared her. They didn't want her around and Ma didn't either—not when they were there. Laine was just a nuisance to Ma's boyfriends, and Ma didn't want them to know she had a half-grown kid.

"Ain't you got nothin' to do?" she'd ask. Laine would go to her room. There wasn't much to do up there, so she'd play with her old doll until she got tired of that, then, if it was summer, look out the window and talk to her flowers.

One Sunday morning, Laine got up for breakfast and found a new boyfriend sitting in a chair in the kitchen. She stopped in the doorway. He was drinking coffee and smoking a cigarette. He had pants on, but no shirt, and he was so thin, Laine could see his ribs.

"Hey, kid, where'd you come from?"

Laine turned to go.

"Don't be shy. Come on in. What's your name?"

"Laine."

"You wanna eat?"

She nodded.

"Well, get what you want."

Laine went in and got her cereal. She sat at the opposite end of the table and watched him as she poured her flakes into a bowl.

"I'm Howie."

Laine picked up her spoon and started to eat.

"Cloris must be your Ma. You look like her. She never told me she had a kid. You're her kid, right?"

Laine nodded.

"How old are you?"

"Ten."

He puffed smoke. Laine lowered her head and concentrated on eating. She could feel him watching her closely.

After breakfast, Laine washed her dishes and put them away. She turned to go.

"Hey, don't go. Stay and talk to me."

She shook her head and ran out of the house. She went to Crystal's but no one was up, so she went to see her flowers.

"Hey kid. Don't go near that house. You'll get hurt," Howie shouted to her from the porch.

She stared at him, but didn't move.

"You hear what I say. Get back here."

Laine knew better than to argue. If she didn't do what Ma's boyfriends said, she got a licking. She came back and sat on a broken chair at the other end of the porch from Howie.

She could hear Ma coming downstairs.

"Howie, you there?" called Ma.

"Out here."

Ma came out on the porch and saw Laine sitting there.

"Ain't you got nothin' to do?" Ma asked.

"Aw, Cloris, leave the kid be. She's fine. You wanna make sure she don't go to that house, though. It ain't safe."

"What you doin' over there?" asked Ma. "You goin' after them damn weeds, ain't you? Well, don't you go no more, y'hear."

Laine nodded.

"Now go play or somethin'."

Laine went up to her room and stared out the window. She figured she'd wait until Howie left and Ma forgot, and then she'd be fine, but Howie started coming over to the house a lot. Sooner or later, Laine knew he'd move in.

Sure enough, one Friday after work, Howie showed up with his car full of stuff.

"Hey kid. What d'you know?" He smiled and handed her a box wrapped in paper with roses on it. "For you. Since we're all goin' to be together, I thought we'd celebrate."

"Thanks," said Laine, taking the box.

"Go on. Open it."

Laine didn't really want to, but he was smiling at her as if he meant it, so she tore it open. It was a pink plastic purse, with a button and loop to close it and a rose for decoration.

"Your Ma said you liked flowers," said Howie.

"But I like dandelions," Laine said, "and the blue ones." She pointed at the burned house.

"But they're weeds."

"I don't care. No one else likes 'em, but I do. I like 'em best."

Laine ran up to her room. She threw the purse on the floor and lay on her bed. She didn't want it. She didn't want Howie. She didn't want anybody.

Howie got a job cleaning school. Laine would see him sweeping the floors before she went home. He'd always call out to her with some message—"Hey kid, tell your Ma I'll be a little late tonight," "Hey kid, your Ma wants you to peel potatoes for supper." The other kids laughed at her. "Guess who Laine's old lady's seein'?" "Hey Laine, wanna stay and help Howie clean floors?"

Even Crystal gave her a hard time, but one day Laine turned on her—"Shut up! Just shut up!"—so Crystal never said another word.

On Saturdays, Howie drank coffee while she ate breakfast and Ma stayed in bed. One morning, Howie put down his coffee cup and looked at her.

"How'd you like to live in a nice place?"

Laine put down her spoon. "What d'you mean?"

"Your Ma and I put in for one of the new houses they're building over by the school. They're real nice. We won't have to live next a burned out piece of junk with trash all over the place and those boys at night.

"No! I don't want to! I want to stay right here!"

"Hey kid, what's your problem? It's not that far, if you wanna see Crystal. You can see Crystal lots."

"No! I won't go! I won't!"

"Shh. Don't wake your Ma."

"I won't!" Laine shouted and ran out of the house. She ran down the street until she ran out of breath.

Eventually, she had to come back. Ma was waiting for her.

"Laine, you get in here this minute. Howie's been tellin' me what you said. You gonna do what we say, y'hear?"

A few weeks later, Howie came home with a key in his hand and a grin on his face.

"Got it!" Howie held up the key. "We move Saturday!" Howie and Ma hugged each other and laughed.

"Who's going to live here?" asked Laine.

"No one, kid. They're gonna knock all these places down and put up apartments."

Laine burst into tears.

"What's the matter with you?" said Ma. "Stop that, y'hear."

But Laine couldn't, so she ran upstairs. She could hear Howie and Ma arguing and then silence.

That night, Laine made a decision. She couldn't do anything about moving or about the houses being knocked down, but she could do something. She could take some flowers with her. The next day, she took a spoon from the kitchen drawer and hid it under her mattress. At night, she lay awake, her heart pounding, until she was sure Howie and Ma were asleep. She crept downstairs and out the front door.

When she got to the burned house, she started digging around the blue daisies, pushing the ground away from the roots. She grew hot and panted with effort. She'd brought a paper bag to put them in and wanted to make sure she got plenty of dirt so they'd live until she got to the new house, but they kept breaking off and she knew they were no good. As she dug around the dandelions, someone grabbed her arm like a vise.

"Hey kid, I thought I told you it ain't safe over here! And at night too!" Howie spoke in a low rumble.

Laine froze, but Howie dragged her to her feet.

"What you doin' here in the middle of the night?" Howie put his face close to hers. "Answer me!"

Laine couldn't. She just stood there until her arm grew so numb, the spoon fell out of her hand to the ground.

Howie looked at it.

"What's all this stuff?" Howie saw the spoon and the bag and the holes in the ground. "What you doing?" He looked at her face. "If I let go, you promise not to run?"

Laine nodded and he loosened his grip.

"Kid, what's with these damn weeds."

"They're not weeds! They're flowers! They're my dandelions and my blue daisies and I want 'em! I don't want 'em knocked down. I want 'em with me!"

"You want dandelions and chicory?"

"Chicory?"

"They ain't blue daisies. They're chicory."

"How d'you know that?"

"Everybody knows that."

"Ma doesn't."

"Well, your Ma's got other things on her mind. Why d'you want 'em anyway? I don't get it."

"They're my friends and I don't wanna leave 'em behind."

"Kid, you're as nuts as your Ma. She ain't gonna like this, you know."

"Yeah, I know."

"Gotta have 'em, huh?"

Laine nodded.

"Well, wait here."

Howie went to his car and came back with a spade from his trunk and a big plastic bag.

"I don't know why I'm doin' this, but here, hold it open."

Howie put the spade to the ground and dug up two large clumps, one dandelion and one chicory. He put them in the bag.

"Come on. Let's go."

They went into the kitchen and Howie put water on them.

Laine grabbed Howie round the waist and gave him a hug.

"Okay. That's enough now. Go to bed."

Laine lay in the dark, the bag by the side of her bed, but then she had to look. She turned on the light and opened it. The chicory was fine, but the dandelions were bleeding milk white where the roots had broken off. Maybe they'd grow, maybe they wouldn't. She'd ask Howie in the morning.

Living Easy

Music drew me to her. Beethoven's Pathétique floated across the marsh backwater from an old clapboard house I thought was empty. Curious, I walked around. By then, all I could hear was birdsong.

When I knocked, I was greeted by an old woman. Her hair was blunt cut, as if she'd done it herself, and a bobby pin held it to one side as if she was a little girl. Although wrinkled, her face had a classic bone structure, but her body was short and square. Thick legs showed beneath a flowered cotton dress, and her bare feet had bunions.

"Hello. I'm Cynthia Malik. I own a cottage on the other side of the marsh. I heard the music and didn't know anyone lived here."

"Moved in last fall," she said. "Want some iced tea?"

"I'd love some."

She headed for the kitchen.

"Watch for Pete. Close the door."

I went in, wondering if Pete was a boy or a dog. Suddenly I realized that I had a bird at my feet, a sparrow with a toothpick tied to his wing. He squawked as I stepped over him. Then I looked up and saw cages with other birds in various broken states—wings, legs, even a beak. The cage doors were all open.

"Here, Petie, Petie," said my hostess. Pete waddled over and climbed on her finger. She put him on the kitchen table, then poured tea.

"Porch?" she asked, pointing to the back of the house.

She spoke in whispers to Pete as we left the kitchen. Her tone was soft and light, her words so quiet I couldn't hear them even though I was right behind her.

The floor slanted to the back of the house. Apart from the cages, all she had in the living room were two wooden rocking chairs and a side-table.

"What brought you to the Irish hills?" I asked.

"Wanted to live easy."

"Have you kept birds long?"

"I don't keep them. They just visit for a while."

I swallowed more tea. Pete stuck his beak in her glass.

"I'm sorry, I don't know your name," I said.

"Millie Aleman."

"I really enjoyed the music. Do you have a large collection?"

She laughed. "No collection!"

"That was you? But I didn't see a piano."

She lifted Pete and got up. "Here," she said, opening the door.

There were two small bedrooms off the back hall. Her bed was in the first, the piano in the second. It was a baby grand and filled the room, but I could see why she'd put it there. The room faced west and south to the sun. There were piles of sheet music stacked on the floor. I started to look through them—classical, modern, broadway, jazz. Most of the modern pieces were original editions.

"Would you play something?" I asked.

"Pick." She put Pete on the piano.

There was so much I wanted to hear, but at last I handed her Debussy's *Images*.

She played *Reflections in the Water*. It was effortless, as if she didn't even have to move her muscles. Her bare bunioned feet looked as if they belonged on the pedals. The music rippled out, and I sat on a pile of sheet music and closed my eyes, drifting away with her.

I don't know how long we sat there after she finished, but I finally opened my eyes. She was looking out the window. The birds were silent in the afternoon heat.

"Thank you. That was wonderful. I must go."

"Come back when you like," she said.

I did. I came back and back and back. We hardly talked, but I felt close to her when she played or when we were silent. We went to Paris, Vienna, the English countryside. We visited Broadway and European cabarets. The birds chattered when I came and were silent when I left.

We never talked about us. It was unimportant if we were married or single, rich or poor, with children or without. It was music and birds.

One day, I was in Mrs. Mullins' general store.

"Haven't seen you in a while," she said, ringing up my groceries.

"I've been busy, and my garden is doing well."

"You seen that old lady out your way?"

"Yes. We've met."

"Don't say much, does she."

"No. She's not much of a talker."

"Must be feeding all the birds in the whole damn county. She buys me out of seed."

Mrs. Mullins knew everyone's habits. She saw what they bought, handled their mail, and got most of the crisis calls if Dr. Bryan was out of town or no one knew what to do.

"You see her much?" she asked.

"Yes."

"How come she's buying bird seed in summer?"

"She helps injured birds."

"She a vet?"

"I don't think so."

Mrs. Mullins snorted. "Sounds like one of those bleeding-heart liberals."

In fall, I realized my concerts were about over. It was time to go back to my teaching job in Dearborn. All winter I wondered about Millie. Her playing was so wonderful, I thought she must have been somebody once, so I went to the library, but I couldn't find anything. I sent her a Christmas card, but she didn't send anything back. I was busy with work and all the unimportant things that seemed to take over my life.

The next summers passed in a dream. I took her vegetables from my garden. She played. Sometimes, I helped with a broken bird. She taught me patience when working with a delicate wren and caution with a raven or hawk. I grew to love summer so much, I could hardly wait for school to end.

The fourth summer, I was hardly in the door before I walked to Millie's, but there was no one there and I couldn't hear anything—no birds, no music. I went to the store.

"Mrs. Mullins," I called.

She waddled out of the back room. "Well, welcome back for the summer. You must be just in. What can I get you?"

"Where's Millie?"

"Who?"

"Millie Aleman."

"Oh, her. They took her away."

"Who? When?"

"The ambulance folk. They showed up asking directions and went out there and took her away. Must of been February, March maybe."

"Where did they take her?"

"Don't know. Didn't say."

"Mrs. Mullins, you know what goes on in this town. What happened to her?"

"I don't know nothing if nobody don't tell me. And nobody didn't tell me nothing."

I could see that Mrs. Mullins' nose was out of joint. I got in touch with Dr. Bryan.

"Her nephew came," he said. "He was upset and asked me to call on her. He said the house was full of wild birds, and she had practically nothing. She didn't say much when I visited, but her nephew was right. The birds had the run of the place. In the end, her nephew found a home for her near where he lives."

"But that's not right! She wanted to stay here."

"But she couldn't take care of herself."

"How do you know that? You didn't even know her. Yes, she takes care of birds, but that's good, isn't it? Have you ever heard her play the piano? She's incredible."

"She didn't have proper heat and she really couldn't take care of herself." Dr. Bryan patted me on the shoulder. "I'm sorry. No one wants to see people in homes, but sometimes it can't be helped."

"That's not good enough. Where is she?"

"I'm not sure I should tell you. Why don't you go home and see how you feel when the shock wears off."

I wasn't getting anywhere, so I went home and worked in the garden, but it was no use. I called him.

"If I promise not to interfere, will you tell me where she is so I can at least visit?" I asked.

She was in a home outside Chicago. Her room was semi-private and she was in a chair, her back to the window, her head on her chest. Her roommate was watching TV.

"Hello, Millie. How are you?"

She raised her head. It took her a moment, then she looked me straight in the eye. "Miserable. Can't stand that," she said, pointing to the TV. Her room-mate glared.

"Oh, Millie, I'm so sorry. How did this happen?"

"I'm an old woman. No power when you're an old woman."

"Why couldn't they leave you alone?"

"Didn't like the way I lived. Wouldn't live like 'normal' people. Besides, I've got money."

"Money?"

"Used to be a concert pianist. Made money then."

"I looked you up in the library, but I couldn't find anything."

"When I quit, I disappeared. Took another name. Not my own, one I made up. My real name's Elizabeth Furman."

I was stunned. Elizabeth Furman! No wonder she played like a dream.

"You had a great career. Why did you stop?"

"Too much pressure. Didn't want it any more. Life was too cluttered. I got rid of things. Fancy house. Furniture. Jewelry. The lot. Bought the house and moved in. Started living easy and felt free as the birds."

"Can I get you anything?"

"Can you get me out of here?"

I didn't know what to say.

She smiled. "You took too long to answer."

I smiled back. "I'll come and see you again."

"No. Just depress yourself. Go home and listen to the birds. Live easy."

I couldn't stop thinking about her. That fall, for the first time, I was glad to close the cottage. Right before Christmas, I got a letter from Mr. Grant, a lawyer. She'd died and left me everything—house, music, birds.

"She never said a word to me," I said to him when I called. "What about her nephew?"

"Her estate is yours. Can we meet?"

I drove to Chicago on a cold, gray day. After we talked, he offered to help me clear things up. We drove to Millie's house.

It was the first time I had approached it from the road, and I was afraid my car wouldn't make it. Mr. Grant unlocked the door and we went in.

Dead birds. Dead birds everywhere, their eyes glassy, lying on their sides in the cages and on the floor. Silent. I felt my knees buckle.

Mr. Grant grabbed my elbow. "Why don't you wait outside while I go through the rest of the house?" I shook my head. In the back bedroom, there was thick dust, and the piano was cold. I lifted the lid and hit a key. Stiff and out of tune.

"Do you play," asked Mr. Grant. I shook my head.

We went into her bedroom, a room I'd only seen from the hall. I opened the closet. A couple of dresses and a coat. One pair of shoes. Her drawers held practically nothing—underwear, a shawl, a photo album. I pulled it out and turned the pages.

How beautiful she was. Her hair was shoulder-length in a page boy style. She wore dresses fitted through the bodice and flared from the waist, and her face had that classic bone structure I'd seen when I first met her.

"I'll get someone to clear things out," said Mr. Grant.

"No," I said. "I'll do it myself."

As soon as I could break ground, I dug a hollow and buried the birds. Then I gave away everything except the piano, the music, and the album.

As summer wore on, I grew more reluctant to sell her house. I couldn't make myself do it. One morning, I walked over there and sat on her front porch, aching for her music. The sun was warm and I drifted into that half-state between waking and sleeping. I thought about her decision to come here, to live easy in this place. Suddenly, I knew that she hadn't played for me. She'd played for the birds. I listened and let their music flow through me.

When I went home, I called the Audubon Society. "How do I start a bird sanctuary?" I asked.

It took two years. I sold the piano and the music for money to keep it going, but not to keep birds. Just to let them visit for a while. Now, I live easy myself.

From Horizontal to Rest

Our children throw balls high in the air
and lose them in the sun.

If so many birds live in the sky,
why don't more fall on our heads when they die?

Why do we celebrate over the dead flesh
and bones of other animals?

We rise with a roar in a hot air balloon
and frighten horses. Then, we float in silence.

What do robins do on rooftops, anyway?
Are they dancing on our graves?

Photo by Rick Smith

Aline Soules writes poetry, fiction, and essays, which have appeared in such publications as *The MacGuffin*, *Detroit Magazine*, *Mobius*, *100 Words*, *Detroit Monthly*, *Sistersong*, and the anthology *Variations on the Ordinary* (Plainview Press, 1995). Some of her short stories and poems have received recognition in contests. She earned a B.A. (Honors) in English with an additional major in Theater Arts, an M.A. in English, and an M.S.L.S. in Library Science. She is also a librarian and has published in library journals, most recently writing a book chapter for *Managing Business Collections in Libraries* (Greenwood Press, 1996). She is currently working on a poetry chapbook which she hopes to complete in 1999.

Miriam Moore, cover artist, paints watercolors and makes artist books in San Antonio, where she is raising two delightful daughters. She has a Bachelor of Arts degree from the University of Texas at San Antonio.

Of "Resting Places," Nancy Ryan's first-place story in the 1996 Detroit Women Writers' Short Story Contest, Charles Baxter, contest judge, wrote . . . *The last two pages of this story were as beautiful as any fiction I've read in the last few weeks: here, setting, theme, and characterization come together with an unusual subtlety and delicacy of feeling.*

Charles Baxter
Author of *Believers*

Ryan's stories are wrapped in domesticities, her main characters connected to and shaped by other family members, missing or present. Her primary theme is relationships, usually within families and among generations, with all the attendant tensions, failures, and joys. In "What Mother Knows," for example, Dara can't acknowledge the strength of her mother's love until her mother is gone, and in "Black Patent Blues," the first-person narrator grapples with the loss of her mother with the help of a mother surrogate.

Stephen Dunning
Author of *To the Beautiful Women*
and *Hunter's Park*

Nancy Ryan's stories and poetry are a blend of pain and rejuvenation. She peels back the surface of her female characters' lives and deftly exposes a range of experience. She mixes the prosaic with the macabre, and the playful with the penetrating to divulge situations that take the reader back and forth in time. Ryan's writing is engaging for anyone who follows "the shape of the heart," with its imposing images and its keen attention to detail.

Conne Hollander
Writer; Faculty, Oakland Community College;
and Coordinator, OCC Writers at Work

This is the first in a series of Plain View Press Flip-books, which combine the work of two writers whose art is closely linked and whose voices complement each other in terms of vision, content, and style.

The Shape of the Heart

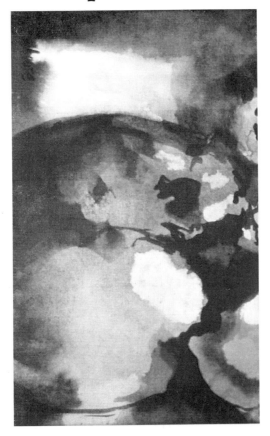

Nancy Ryan

Plain View Press
P.O. 33311
Austin, TX 78764

Phone/Fax: 1-800-878-3605
e-mail: sbpvp@eden.com
http:www.eden.com/~sbpvp

ISBN: 1-891386-06-9
Library of Congress: 99-61023
Copyright: "The Shape of the Heart," Nancy Ryan, 2000. All rights reserved

Acknowledgements

The author wishes to acknowledge the following: "The Nature Area," *The Creative Writer's Craft*, National Textbook Co., Lincolnwood, Illinois, August 1998; "Paralyzed," *The Creative Writer's Craft*; "Frozen Strawberries," *Wild Cat*, Maverick Press, April 1998; "Oakland Mall Elegy," *You're Not Alone*, Citizens Insurance Co. of America, 1997; "Resting Places," First Place, 1996 Detroit Women Writers' Short Story Contest; "Cold Chili," *The MacGuffin*, Spring 1992.

To Bill, who helped give these stories heart. Love you! Nancy

4

This book is dedicated to my mother
Betty Marie Baker Saranen
1926—1988
who showed me the shape of the heart.

Contents

What Mother Knows

"Hear what happened at Redington?" Dara asks her brother, Richard, as they walk Madeira Beach at twilight, with Baby Ali cuddled in Dara's arms. "A bunch of dolphins saved a man being attacked by a shark."

"I try not to think about sharks."

"You should swim with your eyes open. What you can't see can hurt you."

Dara's had enough sharks in her life. One even pulled her leg—here, at this very beach, years ago. She carries the tale, a pale V you feel before you see, on her ankle. "It could have eaten me but didn't," she tells anyone who will listen. "It felt good to walk away."

"I can't stand getting salt water in my eyes," Richard says. "But I have missed the ocean."

"Maybe we could trade houses." Dara slants a glance at Richard, who's spending April with her. "I could live in Detroit; you could live here." She knows Richard will never do this—living in St. Pete means helping their mother, Lorraine, and while the Gulf is a nice place to visit, the nursing home isn't.

"That would mean me getting a new job. You, with your bikini business, can work anywhere."

Dara studies Baby Ali. At two months, she looks more like Lorraine than Dara or Ali's dad, a trucker on the road far more than he's home. Like Lorraine, Ali's cheeks glow conch pink and her eyes mimic the ocean's shifting blue. "True."

This is false. Dara's custom-order bikinis are fun to make and sell well in the sun. She could make custom-order wedding dresses and sell them anywhere, but all that beading takes time. Plus, she likes bikinis; they conceal only what's necessary.

Richard slips off his sandals and walks toward the water, cold for April.

Dara follows him with sandals on. "I'm not sure Lorraine knows you anymore."

"Maybe she doesn't know you either," he says, diving in.

"Maybe." Dara holds Ali above her like a beachball. "I don't know what to do with her. She's as light as Quiche Lorraine."

◯

Lorraine rests in bed 32B, watching Dara bottle-feed Ali in the big oak rocker that belonged to her mother and hers. Listening to Ali's mews for milk, Lorraine pulls her bony knees toward her hips, brings her arms to her ribs, and curls her frail spine. She imagines her own mother's nipple in her parched mouth. Suckling hard, Lorraine gags on spraying milk, milk as warm as the blood the nurse draws every third Thursday. She remembers nursing Dara, who fell asleep five minutes into feedings and woke up a half hour later, wanting more. Richard was as different as a new day, bird mouth gulping sustenance as if her breasts might turn to clay. Both babies thrived, and Lorraine wants so very much to tell Dara this, to tell her to unbind her breasts and throw away her bottles and know what Mother knows, but her tongue won't work.

Lint from Mother's red flannel nightgown works its way into her mouth. Lorraine spits it out, spits out the healthy pudding the nurses feed her, the roast beef and gravy she made every Sunday, the grits she grew up on, too. She has to tell Dara to mother the world, not just Baby Ali, because Dara will need mothering again, too—to give socks to barefoot boys, cream to stray cats, maps to lost travelers. Milk-filled and bursting with breath, Lorraine slumbers in Mother's arms. Someday she'll have to tell Dara these things.

◯

Cradling Ali, Dara sits on Madeira Beach and watches the waves pick up. She remembers shopping at St. Armand's Key with Lorraine before the Alzheimer's got bad, picnicking at Busch Gardens, driving north to Tarpon Springs. Does Lorraine remember any of this, in body if not in mind?

"Brisk," Richard says, drying off and dropping beside Dara on the sand.

"Do as I do. Get some sun."

Dolphins bob a half-mile or so from shore. Dara wishes she could join them. She's read somewhere that a mother dolphin and a midwife nudge each new arrival to the water's surface, where the baby takes its first breath. Without that nudge, the baby sinks.

Lorraine's nudges felt more like shoves in the wrong direction. But Mother Chambers, seventeen years dead, knew how to midwife. And tell folk tales, too. She called Dara a chime child, born between midnight Friday and cock-crow Saturday. "Chime children can see the dead," she'd whisper, "and lead a horse to water and make him drink." "Rubbish," Lorraine would say.

One of the dolphins does a back-flip in the water, as if on command. "What day of the week were you born?" Dara asks Richard, pinching his arm.

Richard raises himself on his elbows and squints, as if trying to see what Dara sees. "Monday, I think."

"Monday's child is fair of face. That's you." Dara continues to watch the dolphins. They remind her of the first summer she spent in Caseville, in Michigan's thumb. There, Lorraine taught Dara to swim, showing her how to doggy-paddle and kick, plunking her in three-foot water, and stepping away. After taking in a tub of water, Dara learned to float, too tired and angry to fear going under. She became a swimmer that summer, and the next summer, when it was Richard's turn, Dara taught him.

Dara kisses Ali's head and holds her tighter. "I can't wait to teach Ali to swim," she tells Richard. "Remember how I taught you?"

"You didn't teach me," he says, throwing a handful of sand at the water. "Lorraine did."

"Little brother," Dara says, shaking her head, "your memory has been edited."

○

Lorraine sits up in bed. Ali's wearing a lilac knit sleeper with "I Love Mommy" embroidered in purple on her chest. Something about it reminds her . . . reminds her . . . reminds her . . . . She must tell Dara to not give away all of Ali's baby clothes after she outgrows them. That's what she did with Dara's, a sure way to have another baby, just like Mother said. She must tell Dara to pull Ali's clothes up over her feet when dressing, not down over her head; Ali will have more time to see the world that way—and it's good luck. She must tell Dara to sing:

Rock-a-bye, baby, thy cradle is green;
Father's a nobleman, Mother's a queen.
Dara's a lady and wears a gold ring;
Richard's a drummer and drums for the king.

Oak leaves fan Lorraine's white wicker cradle, cooling her flushed skin. As the wind picks up, the cradle swooshes to and fro. "High, high, in the sky." Lorraine hears Mother now, and the cradle is a cherry swing. The wind gusts, showering Lorraine with leaves as bronze as Richard's first shoes, and the swing goes higher and higher. When she sees the white gates leading to McKinnons' farm, Lorraine opens her eyes.

She must tell Dara it's easier to swim than sink.

○

The day nurse, Ruth, calls Dara at the condo. "I think you should come right away," she says. "Lorraine said something after breakfast. I think it was 'hell,' but it might have been 'shell.' Did she sometimes say hell?"

"Once or twice. When I married a trucker. And when Richard got Martha Jacobs pregnant."

"Excuse me?"

"It doesn't matter. What matters is that she said something, right?"

"Ruth says Lorraine said 'shell,'" Dara tells Richard when he comes in from his morning stroll. "I think she wants her conch." She walks to the bathroom and removes Lorraine's pink conch shell, a prize from the Florida Keys, from atop the toilet basin.

At the nursing home two hours later, Lorraine rocks and rocks. Dara places the conch on Lorraine's lap. "It's hard to hear here," Lorraine says distinctly, raising the shell to her ear.

Richard kisses the top of her head. "It's me, Lorraine. It's Richard."

Lorraine nods. "Baby Richard. And little Dara."

"Would you like to get out of here for awhile, Lorraine?" Dara asks. "Would you like to go someplace quiet?"

Lorraine nods again, quivery hand touching Ali's cheek.

O

"We could be a postcard," says Dara as Richard wheels Lorraine down the cracked sidewalk bordering Madeira Beach and parks her beneath an umbrella palm. Dara follows behind with Ali in one arm, wicker picnic basket in the other. Beach-goers have come and gone, leaving a multi-colored beachball and footprints in the sand. The footprints could be anyone's—even Dara's, Richard's, or Lorraine's. That's what strikes Dara first, that they've left so many footprints on this beach.

Dara hands Ali to Richard and jogs toward the shore, a lone silhouette against a stringy rhubarb sky. Scores of tan and white shells decorate the sand, but Dara ignores them. She dives in. Surfacing, she eases into the breaststroke. Three-quarters of a mile out, three bottlenose dolphins chirp and whistle at each other. When Dara swims toward them, they chirp and whistle at her, too. She's dreamed of swimming with dolphins, but in her dreams, her arms and legs won't move. This time, knowing Lorraine's watching, she plays follow-the-leader with them, diving, bobbing, and splashing on cue. When a flipper grazes her arm as they frolic underwater, Dara follows the dolphins back to the surface. "Be careful," she thinks she hears Lorraine call, so she waves, treading water. As she nears the shore, she sees Lorraine struggling to sit upright in her wheelchair, trying to wave back.

O

Two days later, at The Tabby Cat in St. Armand's Key, Dara sees a woman who could be Lorraine, flowing white hair bound with a navy and white kerchief, like Lorraine used to wear while gardening. When the woman sees Dara, she stops inspecting a rack of stationery and waves. Dara hurries toward her—how this could be?—but spring-break shoppers block the aisle. By the time Dara reaches the stationery, the woman's gone. After searching the store—no Lorraine lookalike anywhere—Dara buys a package of Siamese notecards. Lorraine loved Siamese cats.

It isn't until the drive home, when she sees Ali's face in the face of the woman at the store, that Dara knows: Lorraine is gone. She drives faster, impatient to pick up Ali, pay the babysitter, and get on home, where Richard waits. She'll rock Ali in her arms, sing her songs in the low pitch of April rain. She'll tell her about Lorraine.

The Nature Area

Three girls sat at the picnic table, finishing their bag lunches.

Carla gazed toward the sugar maple on the edge of the playground. "I love you, Mary Ann," she said, pointing.

That's what someone had scrawled on the paper taped to the maple's trunk, in big block letters: "I love you, Mary Ann." The message was written in magic marker—red, like the tree's October leaves.

Connie giggled. "Wonder who he is."

"I don't care," said Mary Ann.

A boy wearing bright blue pants and carrying a Superman lunchbox sat down by Mary Ann. He handed her his orange. She gave him a yellow apple pale as the noon sun.

"Did you write that?" asked Carla.

"Write what?"

"'I love you, Mary Ann,'" she said, pointing again.

"No." The boy unwrapped his bologna sandwich, peeling away crumpled waxed paper with unsteady fingers.

"Somebody wrote it," said Connie. "Somebody who loves Mary Ann."

"Teddy loves Mary Ann," taunted Carla. "Teddy loves Mary Ann."

Mary Ann pinched Carla's upper arm. "Carla! Leave him alone." She thought about saying so what if Ted wrote it, but she didn't.

Ted rose, shuffled toward the trashcan near the brick schoolhouse, and discarded the waxed paper. On the way back, he tripped over nothing.

"Walk much?" asked Carla.

"No," he answered. "I usually fly."

"That was rude, Carla," said Mary Ann as Ted made his way back to them.

"You're right," said Connie. "We should be nicer." She drew up her knees and rested her chin atop them. "If Ted didn't write 'I Love Mary Ann,' who did?"

Carla shrugged.

Ted ate the yellow apple while Carla and Connie worked their fingers through looped blue yarn, making cats-in-the-cradles and Jacob's ladders. A half-dozen girls jump-roped nearby, and a group of boys arm-wrestled at the other table.

"Do you arm-wrestle, Ted?" asked Connie, trying to be nicer.

Ted blinked. "Not like that."

Mary Ann pulled a string of cherry licorice from her skirt pocket and began chewing on it. "There must be lots of Mary Anns."

Ted spoke. "I only know one."

Carla rolled her eyes, and Connie covered her mouth with her hand.

Mary Ann ignored them. "There must be hundreds of Mary Anns," she said. "In the phone book, for example."

"There must be hundreds of Mary Anns in there," Ted agreed.

Carla smirked. "You don't love people you find in the phone book, Clubfoot."

"Don't call me that."

"Clubfoot. Clubfoot. Clubfoot."

"Stop it," said Mary Ann, standing.

"Stop telling me what to do," Carla told Mary Ann.

Ted stood, too. He pointed at Carla. "You be quiet."

"And if I don't?"

Ted lurched toward her, landing on one knee.

The lunch attendant hurried their way.

Mary Ann threw her licorice onto the ground, marched toward the sugar maple, and sat beneath it, pink-faced.

The lunch attendant helped Ted rise. Near where he'd fallen lay a red magic marker.

"Liar, liar, pants on fire," chanted Carla, and soon most of the other kids joined in, despite the lunch attendant's presence.

"I am not," said Ted, searching out Mary Ann.

Mary Ann avoided his eyes, studying the flowers on her skirt.

"Mary Ann?" asked Ted.

She said nothing, pulling out a new piece of licorice and rolling it between her palms.

Ted made for the back of the playground, walking and then trotting, not tripping once. Then he slipped through the metal gate that separated the playground from the nature area beyond and disappeared.

Connie squinted. "Where is he? Where'd he go?" She looked up, following the vapor trail of a jet in the sky.

Carla picked up the magic marker and put it on the table. "Gone." The other children resumed their jump-roping and arm-wrestling. The lunch attendant looked from the nature area to the sixth-graders she was overseeing. She hurried into the brick schoolhouse, pausing once to glance back, as if unsure what to do.

Mary Ann glanced toward the nature area, too, then at the note on the tree, before rejoining Connie and Carla at the table.

"Have any more licorice?" asked Connie.

Mary Ann gave her a piece.

Carla tapped the table leg with her foot. "Why'd you stick up for him?"

"He's okay. What's wrong with him?"

"Plenty," said Carla.

Mary Ann shook her head. "You don't even know him. He's kinda funny. Really."

Connie looked back up at the sky. "He's different, that's all. You know, spacey."

"I don't like him," said Carla, tearing into the licorice, "and I don't like him at our table."

Mary Ann gave Carla a cool glance, then walked the length of the playground and slipped through the gate. The nature area was overgrown with scrub trees and Scotch pines. There were also a few English hawthorns, and when Mary Ann walked under one of them, a thorn apple bounced off her head.

She picked her way among the trees, looking for Ted. She found him standing beside a pine, arms raised and hands clenched. "What are you doing?" she asked.

"Just being Superman."

"Oh. Are you okay?"

"Sure. Superman's always okay." Ted lowered his arms. "Superman can do anything."

"Not anything."

"Anything."

"Superman knows everything, too," continued Ted, leaning against a lower branch.

"Everything?"

"Everything."

"Does he know who wrote that note?"

"Superman's not saying. But I'll tell you this: Carla is Lex Luther in disguise."

Mary Ann cracked up. "Lex Luther?"

Ted nodded. "When I'm around her, I get weak. Like when Superman gets around Kryptonite."

"That's weird." Mary Ann pulled out her last piece of licorice. "Want it?"

"Yeah," Ted said, but he didn't take it.

"Forget about Carla."

Ted shrugged. "I don't think she likes you, either. She just pretends." He stared up into the sky. "Can you see Krypton?"

"No. The sun's too bright."

"Use your X-ray vision."

"I don't have X-ray vision. Only Superman does."

"Pretend it's night. If you try really hard, you'll see it."

Mary Ann shielded her eyes with both hands and looked up. "I think I see it, Ted. I do. I see it."

"That's the place, Mary Ann. That's where I'm from."

Tara, Obsessed

"What are you?" Mr. Spock said, beaming himself my way.

"A blue M&M."

He looked me over, as if trying to see beneath my tissue-stuffed blue vinyl. "Melts in your mouth, not in your hand."

I rubbed my face with one hand and splayed my grease-paint fingers at him. "Not exactly."

I sighed as he moved away. Not exactly my type.

I followed a gypsy to the bathroom and surveyed the damage. A few strokes of my fingers and my blue face was good as new. When I left the john, Little Red Riding Hood skipped past me and a hooded monk winked, but I saw no other M&Ms. My face and costume started to itch after awhile, and I seriously wished I'd come to the Halloween bash as a nun instead of a piece of candy.

○

I rubbed my eyes, which still stung from last night's makeup, and spilled coffee all over *The Detroit Free Press*, water-damaging everything except the obituaries. So I read them. Read one particular obit till I knew it by heart:

ASHLEY, KAREL BRANTFORD; age 27; Tuesday, October 30, at her Lexington home; beloved wife of Gary; dear daughter of Geoffrey and Sharon; sister of Shelby; "mother" of Olivia and Oscar, Maine Coon cats. Mrs. Ashley will lie in state at Porter's Funeral Home Thursday and Friday from 3-5 and 7-9. To quote Shelby, "Karel expected friends to be numerous and well-dressed."

Between readings, I marveled at the photo of Karel. Dark blonde bob parted on the left and hazel eyes wide, she could have been me.

The people gathered at Porter's Funeral Home two days later saw it the other way: I could have been Karel. Or at least Shelby.

"I'm not . . ." I began as this woman, a baby-boomer in a fitted navy sundress and matching white jacket, vanished into a cloud of people and flower arrangements. There were children, twenty-somethings, baby-boomers, and seniors; gladiolas, chrysanthemums, daffodils, and roses. So many people and flowers I couldn't even see the casket.

Another woman stared at me from behind a spray of mixed carnations. She, too, was wearing navy, but her dress looked like an upside-down tulip.

"You must be Shelby," she said, coming up and squeezing my arm. "I worked with Karel at *The Port Huron Crier*. We'll miss her terribly."

I felt like saying I'd love to work at *The Port Huron Crier*—anything would beat processing returns at Kmart—but I smiled and smoothed my wrinkled peach skirt instead.

An usher walked up and pointed me toward the first row of blue-velour covered chairs. "Those are reserved for family."

"I just want to pay my respects."

"Mrs. Ashley has been cremated," he said. "Would you like to view the photo display?"

"Oh." The obit hadn't said that, but family would have known.

I followed him toward a cherry sideboard: Karel during a piano recital, about seven; in front of the Taj Mahal, a pre-teen; beside a super-jock, sweet sixteen; in cap and gown; in front of a fireplace with two huge cats and a guy who looked a lot like Tom Cruise, just yesterday.

I looked again. And again. Not only did Karel look like me, but the super-jock looked like Mike, my first serious crush. He hadn't been a jock, though. He'd been a freak.

"I can't believe she's gone," a bearded guy told the woman who'd worked with Karel at the paper. "She was born on Houdini's birthday—and died on the anniversary of Elvis' death." His eyes lit up, as if he'd just won a Pulitzer. "Maybe she faked her own death. Wouldn't *that* be a story!"

A woman draped in violet crepe and a stately gray-haired man edged my way. Karel's parents?

"Karel?" The woman veered right, like a driver who'd come this close to being struck by a semi. "You aren't Karel," she said as the man guided her toward a chair.

"I'm sorry . . ." I hurried past her, past the smothering flowers and well-dressed admirers. I couldn't get the old Taurus open fast enough, sure they were after me: Karel's mother and father; Karel's sister and husband, whom I hadn't even met; not to mention Karel herself.

○

In the wintry weeks that followed, I thought about Karel. I wondered if Karel fears the dark, if she imagines dwarves creeping through furnace grates at night. No, Karel's never afraid of anything smaller than herself. I wondered if she wears thermal underwear under silky blouses by day and sleeps in flannel gowns by night. No, Karel always chooses style over comfort. I wondered if she talks too much at large gatherings and not enough at small ones. No, Karel knows exactly how much to say. I wondered why I kept thinking of her in the present tense, when the only sure thing I knew about Karel was that she'd died.

And then one stormy April afternoon, while I was devouring my kiwi and chicken-salad sandwich, Karel struck. Maybe it was because my life was boring, or because I'd never outgrown the game of dress-up. By Memorial Day, my mornings had become Karelesque: Rise at seven and eat Special K with fruit; take a hot shower and final rinse in cool water; allow thirty minutes for clothes and makeup. "Looks aren't everything," I heard her whisper, "but you do clean up well."

By Labor Day, I felt reborn. Tempting fate, I signed up for a Jeffrey Bruce makeover at Glitter Salon. He did radical surgery on the other women but just tweaked me: a few highlights near my face, more subtle eyes. I still had the same boring job, but I spent lunch at the community college library, studying journalism and Maine Coons. I even visited my old veterinarian, hoping to find a Maine Coon breeder. There was a new vet there. He knew a lot about Maine Coons and looked a little like Tom Cruise.

"We've got a stray in the back that needs a nice person like you," he said.

I purred.

○

By October 30, I was in costume panic, remembering last year's Halloween. I was tempted to skip the whole thing this year. I hadn't even found a good costume, bogged down as I was with writing assignments for English 151 and my cat's cold. At first I thought he was just drooling, but when he sneezed all over my comparison/contrast essay, I knew it was time for the vet. Still, Halloween only comes once a year . . . .

"Don't I know you?" a vampire asked soon after I entered the hall, adjusting his cape.

I hunched my shoulders and rolled my eyes.

He squinted, as if trying to figure out what I was.

Body clad in black leotard, pants, and flats and face smeared with white and black grease paint, what else could I be?

"A mime," I mimed.

His face lit with recognition. "Karel Brantford! It's Bob— Bob Brinkley. First-chair trombone, Lake Shore High."

"I'm not Karel," I mimed, pointing my white-gloved hands and shaking my head.

"I sat right behind Jeremy Lindstrom in band. You remember Jeremy, the class clown . . ."

I shook my head and mouthed the words "I'M NOT KAREL."

"It's great to see you—it's been years."

"I'm not Karel," I said, breaking my code of silence.

"Of course you're not Karel. You're a mime."

"I'm not Karel," I said loudly. "My name is Tara, as in *Gone with the Wind*. And no, you don't know me. Unless you go to the community college or return stuff to Kmart frequently."

"Neither. I just moved back here from New York." He stared, as if he couldn't believe I wasn't Karel. "Too bad," he said finally. "I've always wanted to run into Karel Brantford at some party and see if she remembered me."

"Try a ouiji board," I told him, walking away.

"Wait," Bob Brinkley said.

He was tall, dark, and handsome, but I was tired of his pointless banter. I kept walking.

"I really thought you were Karel. Thank God you're not."

That stopped me. "What? I thought you wanted to run into Karel."

"I did. I wanted to show her that one of the guys she called 'loser' did a 100 percent turn."

"She called you a loser? Why?"

"She was a witch. And not just at Halloween."

He said 'witch' casually, but there was anger there and hurt, too. "I take it you didn't like her."

"She didn't like me. She didn't like anybody who didn't shop at Saks."

"She couldn't have been that bad," I said. "She had lots of friends. And she liked cats. People who are monsters don't like cats."

"You knew her, too?"

"I've been mistaken for her before, that's all," I said at last, pulling off one of my gloves.

Paralyzed

Bailey hears the clip of the mare's hooves; sees Shorty's head and neck disappear; feels the reins rip through her fingers and the cow path roll up to meet her. She lies there. She bends her right arm, leans on her elbow, and watches Shorty rise. Front legs splayed, neck bowed, the mare tilts her head from side to side. She looks embarrassed, as if she knows falling on her head is a stupid thing for a horse to do.

The mare begins to graze. Bailey sits up, wondering if she's broken anything. Then she stands. She balances on her right foot, left ankle, knee, and elbow shrieking. Pain. Pain is good. She thinks about trying to get back on but hops Shorty to the barn instead.

In the emergency waiting room, her mom keeps asking what caused the mare to fall. Was the path slippery from the spring rain? Did she trip on something? Did she need new shoes? A sick feeling coats Bailey's stomach. The more her mom questions her, the stronger it becomes. She tries to remember. A black cat crouched in a windrow of the cornfield, tail low. When it pounced, the corn husks crackled. Shorty tensed, but she didn't spook: Her hooves clipped. "We almost somersaulted," Bailey says, starting to cry. "She could have rolled on me." When her mom, pale as a bone, pats her hand, Bailey snatches it away.

The sack-eyed resident who finally checks her out insists that torn ligaments can be as bad as breaks. "How can that be?" Bailey's mom asks. Instead of answering, he tells them to keep her leg up and wrapped, marvels at the healing properties of the young, and promises she'll be back in the saddle soon. Bailey doesn't think so. "We get more people in here from horseback riding accidents than auto accidents," he says, helping her into a wheelchair. Near the front desk, they pass a dark-haired guy in a wheelchair. Only his eyes move. Bailey looks away, right hand reaching for her silver horseshoe.

Listening to "Ghost" on her Indigo Girls CD that night, ace-bandaged leg propped on a pillow, Bailey feels the cow path roll back up to meet her. She overhears her mom on the phone in the kitchen, voice low: No concussion; nothing broken; ligaments. Lig-a-ments. Her mom's voice rises.

"No, I don't know if she got back on . . . ."

It's her dad's guiding principle: If you fall, get right back up.

She can't not hear her mom then. "I don't care if she ever gets back on! I hope she doesn't!"

Ten p.m.—seven West Coast time. Last fall, when Bailey visited her dad in Ventura, she could tell he loved California. Paragliding and surfing were a rush, he said, and the dry heat was good for his old back. Her dad loves rushes. Bailey knows why: It's being on a horse like Shorty, galloping down the back stretch of the track behind the hunt club, hair combed by the wind, eyes streaming. Lost. Found. Lost and found. Bailey rubs her neck. Whiplash? She fingers the silver horseshoe pendant dangling from her neck.

Bailey hobbles to the kitchen. "Mom?" She finds a notepad instead: Her mom's gone to the drug store to get her pain med. When Shorty pulled up lame last winter, Bailey used her allowance to buy Absorbine to rub her down with. It smelled up her jeans and the laundry room, but Shorty got better. Bailey rubs her neck and sits at the kitchen table.

She decides to write her dad and ask how his paragliding business is going. He moved to California the summer before, saying it was a good place to start over. Paradise. Her mom thought he was crazy. She just couldn't understand why people would pay to jump off cliffs in flimsy paragliders. Until this afternoon, Bailey wanted to try it. A bona-fide rush, her dad called it. The best ever.

She picks up the pen and pad her mom left. "There was this black cat," she begins. She knows what her dad will say: Stop blaming the cat. They used to have one, Calico Cally. Whenever a piece of glassware or a knickknack broke, it was Cally's fault. Whenever they ran out of milk, tuna fish, or goldfish crackers, it was her fault, too. And when Freddy Finch had a stroke, Cally was definitely to blame.

Bailey crumples the paper in a ball. She tries again. "I couldn't stop it," she writes. "I've never been so scared." This isn't true: She was more scared when her mom and dad split and kept saying "custody battle" when they thought she wasn't listening. "It wasn't Shorty's fault," she continues, chewing the end of the pen. "And it wasn't mine, either. It was a fluke."

Her mom enters through the side door. "You're still up?"

"It's not me, it's my ghost."

"Not funny," her mom says, handing her a small paper bag. "Go to bed."

Bailey nods, shooing her mom away.

She reads what she's written. "Just ligament damage," she adds. "Lucky me."

Lucky him. What would it take for her dad to give up paragliding? Once, when a strap broke as he soared kite-like ground-ward, he broke three ribs. The worse thing about it, he said, was not being able to deep-breathe. The worse thing would be, Bailey thinks, not being able to breathe at all.

But she can't stop the mantra. Deep-breathing will get you through. Deep-breathing and visualization. Deep-breathing. Visualization. Bailey closes her eyes and breathes deep, imagining she's paragliding atop Shorty, sailing over the cow path, cornfields, and a big black cat. They glide clear across the United States, landing near Ventura. "Glad you came to visit," her dad says. "But where'd you get that cat?"

She holds her breath. "When you were little," her father chides, "you'd do that until you turned blue. You looked putrid in blue. And you'd pass out, too. Deep breathing! Visualization!"

Bailey takes a deeper breath. She's jumping Shorty at the hunt club, the mare's newly shod hooves barely touching down between the white fences. Rounding the back corner of the arena, she sees it: A black cat sitting on the top pole of the final fence. She drives Shorty at it. The black cat hisses. As the mare's head and neck begin to rise, Bailey winks. Out of the corner of her eye, the black cat darts away.

Five Oaks

I.
The oak saplings bent forward,
limbs outstretched like my mother's arms
when I was born.
I heard the brush
of oak leaves against aluminum siding,
rhythmic rustling ushering in sleep.
I remembered leaving
our house on Knollwood Street,
which had no knoll but plenty of woods,
and moving into a tidy brick ranch
next to my grandfather's place,
a cobblestone and mortar fortress
behind a grove of towering oaks.

II.
The oaks told my grandfather stories,
stories he'd sometimes tell me.
Indians once camped in the grove;
bathing in a hole in the creek,
eating wild blackberries and 'coon meat,
sleeping under a canopy of leaves.
He had Indian treasure to prove it—
a weathered Indian whetstone he'd traded
for two loaves of homemade bread.

III.
Tucked into my canopy bed,
I read *Every Child's Encylopedia.*
Genus Querkas, *the oak,*
comes in 300 varieties.
Bartram . . . laurel . . . willow . . .
White . . . black . . . red . . . live.
I read about Annie Oakley, too,

Little Sure Shot,
and Oak Ridge, Tennessee
(see atomic energy and atomic bomb).
The summer of '45,
U-235 production shined at Oak Ridge,
and strontium-90 rained on Hiroshima.
Twenty-five years later,
we still felt the fallout.
Father was a VFW, Mother a pacifist.

IV.
Behind our house, Paint Creek
horseshoed around five grandfather oaks.
I grew up beneath those trees,
playing hide and seek among the trunks,
soaring toward the sky on a green swing,
rolling atop fallen leaves with eager boys.
On wild nights, as we awaited
Father's safe return from the bar,
the oaks shuddered,
flailing branches wailing
like ambulance sirens.
On calmer nights,
as Mother and Father
warmed words by the fire,
I'd gaze above the oaks
at stars bright as Christmas lights.

V.
Some acorns land close to the trunk.
Squirrels steal some away.
Others practice astroprojection.
Grow long, the grandfather oaks whispered.
Live tall. Root yourself in good earth.
My parents died short.
The screech owl in the grove mourned,
and the golden oak floors

squeaked beneath my feet.
Were the trees in color? my grandfather asked.
Was the creek high? Did you see any wild cats?
Yes, I white-lied.
I saw deadwood.
What's left of the rhubarb patch.
A mat of black fur.
I see squirrels climbing the grandfather oaks.
A garden overflowing with Indian corn and tomatoes.
A black cat stalking mice and chipmunks, tail low.
Strong winds roll some acorns home.

Oakland Mall Elegy

On my way to Oakland Mall this morning,
I pass a mailbox hung with black balloons.
A huge sign reads *Happy B-day, Ami,*
and a six-foot cutout says *30.*
It's strung with blinking white lights
and takes me back thirteen years.

They put you in a pink eyelet dress,
placed a bouquet of daisies in your hands,
and laid you in a golden oak casket.
They put tan pancake makeup on your face,
"Bubble Gum" lipgloss on your lips;
you looked like the original Barbie doll.

At the cosmetics' counter at Hudson's,
two teenage girls with teased blonde hair
and tight stonewashed jeans
dip their fingers in lipstick samples,
smear blush on their translucent faces,
and spray each other with Youth Dew.

Our moms told us to learn from your mistakes,
to steer clear of the "three B's": booze, boys, and bad bad girls.
But you weren't a bad girl; even the teachers liked you.
You had it all—money, clothes, blonde hair,
and an imagination that should have been insured
with Lloyd's of London . . . or at least State Farm.

On my way home from Oakland Mall,
I almost miss White Chapel.
Halfway between the Garden of the Resurrection
and the five-foot Memorial Cross, I pull off Crooks Road.
Years have passed since you landed here,
and I haven't visited you once.

We couldn't look your mom in the face.
It must have been her fault.
Why else would you hang yourself
like a bathrobe on a closet rod?
She was the one who'd grounded, grounded, grounded you,
grounded the live wire till, positive energy spent,
your spirit left.

The guy who runs the flower shop
looks you up after I buy a $12.95 bouquet.
Space 4, Section 90. Garden of the Reformation.
But you are lost to me. A security guard
finally finds your grave, on the edge
of Babyland, this side of Reformation.

Ami Ashley—1965-1982.
The wind picks up when I kneel by your grave,
the sun dips a little in the sky,
and I imagine you up there, chatting with Sylvia Plath.

Finally home, I reach
for my high school yearbook and read:
A pale blue dance floor up above;
the doleful cries of a wounded dove.
Wilted daisies in forgotten fields:
Black moons beckon, white suns yield.

And there it is, scrawled on page 225,
right beside a picture of you and Ray
French-kissing at the Valentine's Day Dance:
Only the good die young! Love, Ami (the poet).

Black Patent Blues

Dad pulled the Granada beneath the elm, and we stared at the bare gray farmhouse. We'd lived in that house once, when Dad worked the back acres and Mom worked at the five-and-dime. Before the five-and-dime closed, the yellow paint peeled, and we didn't have enough fives and dimes to buy yellow paint. Before Mom left to play cards in heaven.

"It's going to be tore down," Aunt Flo said, pointing.

I pushed the red balloon Dad got me at the Texaco in town out of the way so I could see. A sign by the porch read "Coming Soon, 'The Garden Place,'" but there were no geraniums in the flower boxes, no pansies in the front bed.

From the looks of it, nobody had lived in the house for awhile. Black plastic covered the upstairs windows, but the kitchen and living room ones stared back at us, unseeing eyes. We got out of the car and walked toward them: It was okay to look in nobody's windows.

"We should have stayed," I told Dad.

"You gotta let things go."

Aunt Flo snorted. It was the one thing she did real well. When she snorted, it was like a stream of dirty words came flowing from her nose. Dad would shut up then, even if Aunt Flo didn't tell him to.

I tried to snort too.

"What?" Aunt Flo looked hard at me. "You're not crying, baby?"

I pressed my forehead against the cloudy living room window and peered in. The wood floors, which Mom used to wipe down with mineral spirits, were dirt-covered.

Dad cleared his throat. "Maybe they'll keep plants in there, so they won't freeze."

"Tssk," Aunt Flo said. She marched to the back door and rattled the knob until it opened. Mom was always on Dad to fix that knob.

Aunt Flo pulled a broom and rag out of the back closet and handed them to Dad and me. Then she picked up Mom's dustmop and shook it.

While Dad wiped the windowsills, I danced around the living room, sweeping dirt on my brown tassel loafers. Aunt Flo said she'd found the shoes at the dry cleaners in Port Huron where she worked. That somebody left them on the counter and never came back. "Perfectly good and clean," Aunt Flo said, giving them to me.

When we lived in this house—when Mom was still with us—I lost my black patent shoes in the park behind Clark's Groceries. Mom and Aunt Flo went to town to get pot roast and vegetables for dinner. I hated pot roast because it meant leftover onions, so I went to the park, took my shoes off, and climbed the willow.

When I got down, my shoes were gone.

"I told you not to wear your good shoes," Mom said. "They're your favorites."

"Shut up," Aunt Flo told her. I felt like saying the same thing. They were my favorites; that's why I was wearing them. They were so shiny your eyes glistened when you looked in them.

I stopped and looked down at the loafers, imagining they were Dorothy's ruby slippers. That reminded me of Casey—half-terrier, half-collie—slipping through Mom's legs when the back door opened and tearing down Tyson Rd. I'd charge after him, but Casey must have kept a map in his head. He always came back.

I clicked my heels together: *There's no place like home, there's no place like home.*

I swept the dirt into a little pile in the corner where the TV used to be, then stopped again. Mom used to keep a picture of her, Dad, and me on the TV. Aunt Flo took it at the Fishfly Festival. We had pink cotton candy stuck to our faces. But what I remember most about that picture was Mom looking like she knew something we didn't.

Aunt Flo leaned on her dustmop. "Come on, Cinderella. Snap to."

"What?"

"Cora Blue!" Aunt Flo snapped her fingers.

My full name. I knew I was courting trouble, but I clicked my heels harder. "Why do we have to clean? It's going to be tore down anyway."

Aunt Flo gave Dad her disgusted look. "Respect."

That word again. Dad said he respected Aunt Flo—she was Mom's big sister and just look at all she'd done for us—but I think he respected her snort.

"Why?" I asked again.

Dad scrunched his lips together. "Respect!" I could almost hear him say.

I swept myself toward him. "I don't get it," I whispered.

"You don't need to get it," he whispered back. "Just sweep."

"I'm going upstairs," Aunt Flo said. "To see your momma's room one last time. Your momma had the nicest room."

Mom's *sick* room was what she meant. We never called it that, though. We made it all pink and white and pretty, pasting paper roses from magazines to the walls and putting fresh daisies in mason-jar vases.

Dad and I watched her go. "I'm tired of sweeping," I said when she reached the top step.

"Sweep."

I leaned against the cold plaster wall. "Why does she want us to clean?"

Dad swiped at a cobweb dangling from the side window. "Your mother loved this house."

"That's why? For Mom?"

"Something like that."

Aunt Flo's feet scraped the floor above us.

"Flo," Dad called a minute later. "Maybe we should go. We don't own the place anymore, you know . . . "

I was thinking the same thing. What if the police came? I hated sirens. The morning Mom died, the front yard was full of them. An ambulance and two police cars. One of the policemen gave me a fuzzy brown bear to hold while another policeman spoke to Dad.

"Why didn't you call a doctor?" I thought he asked.

"Too late for that," I thought Dad answered.

"Did you know she was dying?" I thought he asked.

"She knew," I whispered.

Aunt Flo came to the top of the stairs, dustmop held like a rifle. "It's better now," she said.

"Can we go?" I'm not sure who I was asking. Dad or Aunt Flo? Mom?

Dad said yes; Aunt Flo just nodded.

I followed them to the Granada and climbed into the back seat. The red balloon from the Texaco floated past Aunt Flo.

"Grab it!" I yelled, but she was busy dabbing her eyes.

I jumped out of the car and into the air, reaching for the red-ribbon streamer. The balloon was already high above me, above the empty house and untended fields. Going higher. Floating away.

Aunt Flo got out of the car and stood beside me. "Don't think twice about that balloon," she said, hugging me tight. "It's headed straight for your momma."

I sniffled, but I didn't cry.

"Cora Blue," Aunt Flo said. "Did you just snort?"

I hugged her back.

Sourdough

I was a chubby kid, and it had as much to do with Mrs. Hyke's sourdough biscuits as it did Grandma's homemade bread. They both made gingerbread, too—served warm with hard sauce at Grandma's, cold with whipped cream at Mrs. Hyke's. Grandma watched me on Tuesday and Thursday afternoons; Mrs. Hyke on Monday, Wednesday, and Fridays. Although I never told Grandma, Mrs. Hyke's gingerbread outdid hers: You could press the crumbs together until they formed one last luscious bite. Mrs. Hyke's biscuits had more tang than Grandma's bread, too. But the bread had more staying power.

I'd had my fill of that which didn't stay. First Father. He died early, when I was five. Cancer. Of the skin. Mother took on a string of odd jobs and men after that: Kresge's, Woodward Cleaners, Jimmy's Coney Island (my favorite restaurant); Mr. Porter, Big Ben, Uncle Jim (my favorite uncle). We never stayed in one place long—we got around.

Love was homemade bread and biscuits, I decided in my fourth-grade year. I knew Grandma loved me—she had a bad heart, but it was big—and I guessed Mrs. Hyke did, too. On days I really needed sourdough biscuits she made them, as if reading my mind. Years later, when Grandma told me that Mrs. Hyke once had a husband and four children, but they'd died in an early morning fire New Year's Day 1955, I wasn't even surprised. I'd guessed that she'd known sorrow—I'd known sorrow, too. Those sourdough biscuits were her way of working it through. As she kneaded the dough, her hopes and dreams would rise. And when I smiled at her, she'd see the goodness and love of those four children.

Sometimes I wondered how she went on at all. Didn't she just want to burn up, too? But then I'd see her dousing herself with flour—dumping it here, dusting it there—and reveling in the smell of baking sourdough.

Her husband started the fire, Grandma said, carelessly, by dropping a cigarette between two couch cushions. I could picture it, that hope, those dreams: Mrs. Hyke in a teal taffeta dress—teal was her best color—drinking spiced cider, eating skewered Spanish olives and cocktail sausages wrapped with cheese, ringing in the new. Afterward, she kissed each child goodnight and made love with her red-eyed husband, the careless one. He fell into a black sleep; she couldn't. When the fire started, she tried to rouse him. She couldn't. She tried to carry each child out . . . but couldn't. She couldn't decide which child to pick up first, she loved each one so much. So she stayed, rooted to the house where she'd washed diapers and scraped baby food off walls, inhaling smoke and trying to extinguish fire.

That's how I imagined it. One thing's for certain. Mrs. Hyke should have died, too. But she couldn't: Years later, I'd need her to love me.

Sometimes both Grandma and Mrs. Hyke watched me on Friday and Saturday nights. Actually, I watched them play euchre for money; Mrs. Hyke usually won. "Now don't get too excited, Edie," she'd tell Grandma before dealing, and Grandma would giggle. On those nights, Mother waited tables at The Four Corners. "The easy easy," she called it. Food that was easy to eat and serve, drinks that eased men's wallets. A good Friday night netted some $45 in tips, a great Saturday night, $75. One good night followed by one great and Mother would buy a new outfit for Malibu Barbie, my favorite doll.

I loved to dress her in hot pink or tango orange, bright colors that showed off her tan. I especially loved her in hot pink hot pants with white knee-high go-go boots. I'd have done anything for a tan and legs like hers. Except give up sourdough biscuits. "My feet would hurt if they were shaped like hers," Mrs. Hyke said when I mourned my size-eight feet. She didn't think much of Barbie's waist, either. "She looks pinched," she said. "And hungry." Mother said my waist would never look like Barbie's if I kept eating Mrs. Hyke's sourdough biscuits, but Mother's waist didn't look like Barbie's either, and Mrs. Hyke and I never left her any biscuits to eat.

For my twelfth birthday, Mrs. Hyke gave me a "Campus Queen" lunch box, white with lavender trim. Campus Queen wore a strapless pink gown and a sparkly tiara. I already had breasts, but they weren't pointy like Campus Queen's and would never hold up that dress, and I had a feeling the tiara wouldn't stay on my head any better than the book Mother put there to improve my posture. Campus Queen's feet looked suspiciously like Barbie's, so I thought it was awfully nice of Mrs. Hyke to buy the lunch box for me. She was feeding my hopes and dreams—though we both knew I'd never be Campus Queen.

When I turned thirteen, Mrs. Hyke left Detroit for Scottsdale, Arizona. If it wasn't for us and congenital heart failure, Grandma surely would have flown southwest with her. "It'll be better for her arthritis," Grandma said, sniffling. When good-bye time came, Mrs. Hyke cried outright. "For my big girl," she said, pressing a white leather ring box in my hand. Inside were two of her rings: a one-carat cubic zirconia and a heart-shaped amethyst. As she hobbled out of our brownstone on her drugstore cane, I hoped Scottsdale would be to her legs' liking. Hoped but wondered: How would we survive without her?

We more or less did. Mother gave up her Friday and Saturday night job for a small-time jeweler named Harley Dietz, one of the men with the easy wallets she'd met at The Four Corners. Grandma found a new euchre partner, a blue-hair named Alice, although her failing heart wasn't in it. I, now a teenager, took to watching myself after school . . . and to watching Mother. Twice I'd caught her wearing my rings from Mrs. Hyke. All I could think was that she'd lose them somehow. She might give them to Harley Dietz to sell or take them off to make pizza dough, her new fascination.

Mother's pizza always stuck to the pan. She'd make two pizzas at a time—one to eat then, one to freeze for later. She'd flip the dough into the air like she saw some chef do on TV—and then forget to oil the pan. I wrote Mrs. Hyke and told her about this. "Be kind to your mother," she wrote back, "she works hard." I didn't hear from her after that. My letters came back "Unable to deliver. Return to sender"—even the one telling her Grandma's big heart had finally failed to beat—so I figured she'd died, too. But five years later, I got a call from this lawyer who called himself Mrs. Hyke's stepson. Mrs. Hyke had died in Phoenix, he said. She'd married his father, Henry Mitchell II, an Arabian horse breeder with three sons. Mrs. Hyke (Mrs. Mitchell) had provided for me in her will; a check for $25,000 was in the mail.

I gave half the money to Mother. A month after that, her hopes and dreams rose, too. She and Harley married small and honeymooned big: Once the justice of the peace blessed them, they were cruising to the Cayman Islands. I never asked who paid for the trip—I could guess. Mother wanted to take my rings with her. I said no, hiding them in Malibu Barbie's traveling case a week before the wedding. She wasn't going anywhere.

"Forcynthia"

The envelope had no return address. When Margery opened it, a piece of lavender stationery and a photo of Cynthia and J.T. in front of a colonial-red farmhouse fell out. "Dear Margery," the letter read, "We haven't kept in good touch, but I wanted you to know. We're back in the area: 2221 Barnes Lake Rd. Please call. Or just stop by. Love, Cynthia. P.S. J.T.'s been asking about you."

Margery sat on the big rock near the forsythia and remembered . . . the summer of '71—the summer before Jimmy was drafted. That summer, The Reverend Jones disowned his own daughter, Cynthia, for getting it on with every boy in town, and she moved out of the rectory and in with Margery and and her precious son, Jimmy. That summer, Jimmy fixed Cynthia fresh orange juice and omelets every morning and brought her dandelions and daisies every night. She braided the daisies into her long brown hair but left the dandelions on the counter for Margery, who hated dandelions almost as much as she hated Cynthia Jones.

Then Jimmy began planting things for Cynthia. He turned up a 12' x 12' plot near Margery's chrysanthemum bed and filled it with tomatoes, green peppers, zucchini, and pea pods. He painted the spare bedroom celery green and bought a "forcynthia" bush to go beneath the bedroom window.

"Forsythia," Margery had corrected as Jimmy and Cynthia chased each other around. "Forsythia."

Margery plucked a dead leaf from the forsythia. It had yielded yellow flowers each spring for twenty-one years, but she'd never cut it back. The bush stood six feet now and was nearly as wide, and its long arcing branches had finally refused to bud.

She rose, walking to the chrysanthemum bed to pluck a milky blossom. Suddenly she was back in the maternity ward with Cynthia, who was gushing J.T. this and J.T. that. Buried within swaddling clothes, James Taylor Wade, Jr., looked more like an old man than a newborn—and nothing like his namesake. White wisps fringed his translucent skull, his watery eyes seldom opened, and he coughed when he cried.

Margery sighed, remembering how she'd tried to look through the newborn, sure the marrow beneath his skin, muscle, and bone held the truth. When that didn't work, she traced the veins on his puny arms, hoping to read them the way fortune tellers read palms. And when that didn't work, she trusted her heart: Her Jimmy wasn't this sickly baby's father.

All Margery could think about was how she herself lay in bed for three months straight when carrying Jimmy. Hand on her belly, she'd feel the life within her grow stronger. Her body was the sea; her veins, rivers carrying water to the source of life. Lifeboats brought food to it; dolphins protected it from sharks. Then one day the sea parted, leaving a towhead baby boy in its wake: James Taylor Wade.

Margery studied the photo. Cynthia looked as waif-like as ever, but J.T. had changed. He did look a bit like Jimmy, with those broad shoulders, perry-boulder blues, and golden-brown curls. Margery stuffed the letter and photo back into the envelope. She'd written occasionally as Cynthia moved from town to town and man to man, but Cynthia was right: They hadn't been in touch. I'll just stop by, like the letter says, Margery thought. Stop by and leave.

O

The next morning, Margery placed the letter from Cynthia on the passenger seat of her blue Impala and drove toward Barnes Lake. Dusty road signs, brown-needled pine trees, rusty mailboxes, and an occasional dog blurred by, but no red farmhouse. Margery pulled into the nearest driveway, put the Impala in reverse, and hit the brakes. A pale-pink two-story farmhouse with baby-blue shutters and white gingerbread trim loomed before her. A slate sign hung in its picture window, surrounded by those blinking Christmas lights Margery had always hated. "Oh, my God," she whispered, peering over her glasses. "'Jimmy Wade's Cafe. Great Breakfasts Any Time of Day.'"

Margery parked the Impala on an angle and pulled herself out of it. A small sign read "Open for Business," and two waitresses in French-maid costumes milled about the front tables. The wooden screen door eased closed behind her, as if recently planed and oiled.

"I'm here to see Cynthia Jones," Margery told the closest waitress, a skinny brunette with raccoon eyes.

"Cynthia," the waitress yelled.

A tiny redhead in a starched apron and chef's hat stepped from behind the kitchen counter. "Margery? I can't believe it!"

"Me either," Margery said, eyeing the cafe's tiered muslin curtains, floral wallpaper, and white-clothed tables.

"I can't believe you came," Cynthia said, pecking Margery's cheek. "J.T. will be thrilled. Have a seat . . . . Want a cup of coffee?"

Margery wedged herself into a chair. "Jimmy Wade's Cafe? What were you thinking?"

"Remember how Jimmy always wanted his own little restaurant?" Cynthia asked, sitting kitty-corner from Margery. "I did it for him."

"You could have at least left it red," Margery said as the waitress served coffee and a plate of fancy pastries. "Jimmy's favorite color was red." She tried to think of something else to say, but the thought of a frilly French cafe with Jimmy's name on it left her speechless.

Cynthia peered over her coffee cup at Margery. "I dreamed about Jimmy one night last spring. His plane was flying real low, but instead of crashing in Vietnam, it set down ever so softly in a big green field." She lowered the cup to the table, mimicking the landing. "And when I woke up, he spoke to me. 'Open up a little cafe that serves all different kinds of omelets,' he said. And that's what I did. We have broccoli and cheese omelets, beef and Philly omelets, Denver omelets . . . ."

"Denver omelets?" Margery asked, recovering her voice. "Jimmy never went to Denver."

"Ham, dill pickles, and Swiss. It's our specialty. Want one?"

Margery shook her head, scanning the menu. "'Jimmy's Coney Island.' What's that?"

"Chili, onions, and cheddar."

Margery slapped the table with both hands. "Jimmy never made that."

"I never said he did."

"You did so. You named this place 'Jimmy Wade's Cafe' and that omelet 'Jimmy's Coney Island.'"

Cynthia rearranged the silverware before her.

"You bought this place on the basis of a dream?"

"Leased it. I've had it with waitressing, Margery. Serving burgers and smiles to big businessmen and rabbit food and Chardonnay to their little wives. I've done my time."

"Who's paying the bills?"

"I am. We've only been open two weeks, but the word's getting out. People will come, like Jimmy said."

Margery picked a white chocolate eclair from the pastry plate. "*Field of Dreams*, huh?"

"Good movie."

The voice wasn't Jimmy's, but the head and shoulders were. Margery grasped the table. She tried to remember the last time she'd seen J.T. She'd received an invite to his high school graduation, but she'd already bought tickets to the Meadow Brook Lawn & Garden Show. It must have been his sixteenth birthday, when Cynthia had melted the baked Alaska.

"J.T., you remember Margery," Cynthia said. "Grandma Wade, I mean."

"Hi," he said.

Cynthia rose from the table and hugged J.T. "I'm going to make your grandma a Denver omelet," she said, scurrying toward the kitchen. "You entertain her."

Margery cleared her throat. "Good to see you, J.T."

"Same." J.T. plopped into Cynthia's seat, put his right foot on the table, and leaned forward to tie his sneaker.

The sight of J.T. hunched over his shoe like that reminded Margery of Jimmy: the white shoes he'd worn as a toddler and how he'd raised his little feet to his mouth and chewed on the laces.

"Nice shoes," she said as J.T. looked up.

"Thanks."

Margery tried again. "So you're all grown up. What's next?"

"Didn't Mom tell you? She tells everybody. Thinks I'm crazy."

"Tell me what?"

"I'm short two dogs. As soon as I find them, we're out of here."

"Your mother's moving again?"

"Not her. Me and the dogs. I'm gonna start a dog-sledding business in the U.P. Take tourists into the tundra for $100 a head."

Margery pierced the eclair with her fork. "People would pay to go dog-sledding in the middle of nowhere?"

"Sure. Adventure vacations are in."

"Isn't life adventure enough?"

"Not at Jimmy Wade's Cafe. I'm not spending the rest of my life flipping omelets, Margery."

○

Cynthia returned a few minutes later with Margery's Denver omelette.

Margery ignored it. "So J.T.'s leaving?"

"He told you? About the crazy dog scheme?" Cynthia swept chocolate-cake crumbs off the table with one hand and swooped up a folded newspaper with the other.

Margery snatched the newspaper and began reading the travel section. "'Hurricane damage is everywhere, but Hawaii's re-blooming beauty and empty beaches make it an ideal vacation getaway,'" she read aloud.

Cynthia walked behind the snack bar and began wiping it with a wet dishrag. "That's it! The 'Maui Wowee'—pineapple, ham, and cream cheese."

I feel like an old volcano, Margery thought, an old volcano with red cinder cones on its lips, like Mount Haleakala. "Omelet or pastry?"

"Omelet, of course. Jimmy would have loved it."

"Jimmy would have hated it. He didn't like pineapple. And he hated cream cheese."

Cynthia rounded the snack bar with the dishrag. "He did not. He loved cream cheese almost as much as he loved me."

"Jimmy hated cream cheese."

"How could he hate cream cheese and love cheesecake? Tell me that."

Margery snorted. "The only cheesecake Jimmy liked had girls like you on it."

The dishrag hit Margery's left cheek, assaulting her with fried egg and Lemon Scent Dawn.

"Jimmy didn't consider me cheesecake. He wanted to marry me and be a family."

"Jimmy had a family. And if it wasn't for you, he'd have gone to college. He wouldn't have gone to Vietnam at all. And he wouldn't have . . ." She paused, out of breath.

"Jimmy didn't want to go to college, Margery. He wanted to open a place like this one. That's why I got pregnant."

Margery stood. "You 'got pregnant' because you slept with half the town."

"Says who? You?"

"Says your father. I don't blame him for kicking you out. I just can't believe I took you in."

"My father didn't kick me out. I left so he'd stop—God—it's none of your business. And you hardly took me in. You put up with me, the way you'd put up with any stray Jimmy brought home." Cynthia rushed past Margery and out the door, slamming it shut.

Margery dropped into the chair. The volcano was quiet now, and Margery was, too. She jumped when another door slammed and an engine growled, then slumped forward. She'd waited more than twenty years to put Cynthia in her place, and she'd never felt worse. Jimmy hadn't been sold on the idea of college; it was more her idea than his. And Reverend Jones had always given her the creeps . . . .

Closing her eyes, Margery remembered the bountiful breakfasts Jimmy had made for Cynthia and how he'd touched Cynthia's hair before boarding the plane for Vietnam. She remembered how safe that plane had seemed, as safe as a mother's womb, and how Jimmy had waved at her and Cynthia from the window before takeoff. And she remembered how, after the letter came from Washington and memory was all that was left of Jimmy, Cynthia wrote his name on scrap paper, grocery lists, even cardboard boxes, and how it so infuriated Margery that she'd asked Cynthia to leave.

J.T. sauntered back into the room. "Where's Mom?"

"Not here," Margery mumbled.

"Where'd she go?"

"Where does she go to be alone?"

"To church."

"Church?"

"The Presbyterian around the corner. Sometimes she prays for my dad. Like he's coming back."

Margery rested her head on the back of the chair. Washington said he wasn't coming back, but Margery could almost see him, getting off a Boeing 757 at Metro Airport and running toward her, immune to powder burn and aging. He'd looked like J.T., and when he'd say he wanted to marry Cynthia, Margery would tell him how she'd kept his dream alive . . . .

"No," Margery said aloud. "No more dreaming." She saw Jimmy's plane crash in a forest of steaming vegetation, heard a battery of shellfire, felt the shrapnel pierce his side. Tears collected in the corners of her eyes. Cynthia wrote that J.T. had been asking for her, but Margery knew better. "Tell your mother I'm sorry," she said, pulling the Impala keys out of her purse.

○

That fall, as the sugar maples dotting Margery's backyard turned red as cinnamon candy and Canada geese salt-and-peppered the golf course next door, Margery snipped and clipped the forsythia into shape. Day by day, she sculpted away, digging up old roots and storing them in a brown burlap bag. Three weeks before Thanksgiving, while Margery was finishing the forsythia, another letter came. J.T. had found the missing links to his dog-sled team, Cynthia wrote, and moved to Rudyard, just above the Soo. But business was good at Jimmy Wade's Cafe, so she was going to stay. And the Maui Wowee was a big hit.

Margery sat on the big rock by the chrysanthemum bed and reread the letter, amazed that Cynthia had again forgiven her. She knew Cynthia would be lonely on Thanksgiving and made a mental note to call her. Why, she'd even . . . Margery reached into the burlap bag and pulled out a forsythia root. Kneeling, she brushed dead grass and leaves from the early November ground, clearing a place.

Frozen Strawberries

I.   My mother didn't like it, but on Saturdays, just before closing time, we'd stop by Bud's Best Cars and test-drive the new used cars. Once, we got pulled over in a black '68 GTO for going ten above. My father tried to weasel out of a ticket, telling the cop the speedometer was busted and the GTO wasn't even ours; I wrote "I love you" with Berry Breeze lipstick on the rear seat. When Mother asked who'd done it, Father winked.

II.   The cowboy tossed me my purse, a beaded bag made from recycled Lee jeans; the strap hooked around the horn of the western saddle, keys, makeup, and wallet slapping Big Red's withers. He shied sideways. The purse slapped again, and the strawberry roan was off, bucking like the rodeo bronc he wasn't. I landed on my butt in six inches of prairie grass, still holding the reins. "I'll teach you how to fall," the cowboy said, picking me up.

III.   We feasted on Dover Cream and wild strawberries, perfectly halved, at a tiny dairy some twenty miles from Buckingham Palace. "London Bridge is falling down," he whispered, "we'll have to stay." We viewed the giant panda exhibit and caught an auction at Sotheby's. "The Berlin Wall is falling down," he whispered, "we'll have to go." The wishing well inside me, dehydrated for twenty years, overflowed. I was Pegasus, flying from England to Germany when we could have taken the ferry. We hugged the curves of the Autobahn, downed pink champagne in black patent pumps, and licked powdered sugar off angel wings, body-slamming into the ground where the wall had been. I awoke. Alone.

IV.   The night before she died, my mother sat on a bench outside Baskin-Robbins and created a pink ice-cream pyramid that diminished in size but not shape until it disappeared. I felt like that when I found her. Her body had retained some warmth, but her fingers were blue-moon cool. I did what the caring do at the end of the movie: One hand on the bed to steady myself, I closed her eyes.

V. My mother made strawberry pie crisscrossed with whipping cream; I swirled rebellion in her latticework. "Strawberry shortcake," my father said, "you're a peach." A red roan bucked me off; I hopped back on and rode him hard. I kissed the strawberry mark on my lover's back and inhaled his fruity aroma. And fell again. Then I learned. When he lied to me like that, I could have ripped his heart out and put it on a paper plate. Mother said, "Cancerous: I told you so," consuming bowls of strawberry ice cream when the doctor ordered more tests. Motherless, I tied a six-foot string to my tooth, placed a frozen strawberry in my mouth, and backed away from the door. Then I knew. When you pick strawberries with your eyes closed, time withers. I saw the limp leaves, the fleshy stems of what was. The Beatles were wrong.

Heartwood

Estate sale: January 31, 1997

Postcards from my father, who forsook love of two women for love of the redwoods, take little space. Maybe he died there, puffing Camels beneath a dry California sky. I know he died here, leaving a mother who spoke only Spanish and my mother, who never spoke his name. Mother's pecan dining table takes the most room. She waited tables for a table but got me instead. When Grandpa bought the table, Mother stayed home, polishing it daily with one of my cotton diapers. It's quite a burden, to be upstaged by a table, but I got over it.

As strangers sift the other items, time slides by.

1930

I get my first pair of glasses, brown half-moon frames with myopic lenses. Bridget the Brittany flushes pheasants from the field where Grandpa runs her; Grandpa takes a swig of Wild Turkey when he thinks nobody's looking. Mother trades kisses with the bald man who owns the dairy next door. "Mr. Patterson," she says, tousling my hair. "Wild Bill," he adds, winking. Mother says I have to like him: He gives us free milk. I vow never and run away, hiding in the barn until feeding time.

1941

Mother forsakes love forever and buys a boarding house filled with milk glass in Port Huron. Three months later, she meets and marries Billy Taylor, who says he's a fireman but isn't. I go with him to play donkey baseball—all these big guys astride little donkeys, bats high. Charley LeGuin, the blue team's pitcher, is minus two fingers on his right hand. This is why I marry him. We buy a bungalow on twenty acres in Lapeer, cheap. Grandpa shoots his foot instead of a pheasant, a wound that won't heal, and loses his leg. We transplant two evergreens from Grandpa's farm and one shoot from his shagbark hickory.

1949

Inside a red and gold box that once held Chinese tea, I save two packs of matches: one from Mother's wedding to Billy Taylor, one from mine and Charley's. The box's *fleur-de-lis* foil crackles, and the smoky odor inside carries across the fishing pond to the railroad tracks beyond. There, on brush-covered banks dried by drought, sparks from the four a.m. freight train smolder, ignite, explode. Charley sees the fire first, from the upper bedroom window, a chain of orange and red flame rolling our way. "What if it crosses the pond?" I ask. "Can't walk on water," he promises. But Charley forgets things, like the snow fence he put around the pond two winters ago. Hidden by milkweed and cattail husks, the fence waits. When the chain of flame comes, it halos the pond, like the gold-leaf frame around Mother's favorite mirror. In it, I see Mother and Billy Taylor burning; their marriage, ashes.

1965

Arrows fly. The creek behind the house flows fast, brown as falling leaves. Atop those leaves, a twelve-point buck bleeds slow through a dime-sized hole. I watch from my bedroom window and know: The old man next door is poaching again. I call the township hall and report him. Five minutes later, Charley saunters in. "Got one," he brags, his bow held up like a trophy. Grandpa dies slower. Cancer.

1977

We visit Sarasota. Barnum & Bailey, art fairs, salt water stinging my eyes. I buy a shellacked black box, inlaid with mother of pearl. Inside, I put twenty-five sand dollars: some smooth as soap; others gritty, like the earth from which they came.

1980

Wild Bill Patterson comes to MacCauley's Funeral Home to visit Mother. He leaves us a vintage milk bottle from The Oak Dairy. "Nice man," Charley says. "A lot nicer than Billy Taylor," I say. Spilt milk.

1995

The shagbark hickory Charley and I planted in '42 is near one-hundred feet now, and half the bark is gone. The other half is hanging on like the dying when near ready to go. Soon the hickory will be naked, with all the white sapwood exposed. Then they'll split the sapwood, baring the red-brown core beneath. The heartwood.

As I trek from the house to the mailbox, I lean on a hickory walking stick, from a shoot of the shagbark hickory. The walking stick's handle, a deer antler with a whistle carved in it, softens my hand. When I grasp it, I see Charley. He's at MacCauley's. He sits up when I walk in, swings his spindly legs over the casket, and crawls toward me. "I can't find my wallet," he sobs, "or my car. Where's my wallet? Where's my car?"

February 1, 1997

The garage behind the shagbark hickory is empty now, save Charley's rusted-out blue Bonneville. Two more days of estate sales, and this house will be empty, too. I'll send postcards from Sarasota.

Cold Chili

Mona crouches beside the chili-stained wall, sponge in her left hand, cleanser in her right, and surveys the aftermath of today's bout with Sean, her five-year-old son. "You were very bad today," she tells him. But the little boy upstairs can't hear her. "Just wait until Daddy gets home," she says, louder. He won't hear this, either; he hardly ever hears her, not even when he's in the same room. She attacks the wall, trying to remove every trace of beans, sauce, and broken bowl—and the anger her own flesh and blood provoked. It's not his fault, she tells herself finally, he doesn't mean to be bad.

"Attention-deficit hyperactivity disorder," Dr. Schaefer said after seeing Sean for the third time and consulting with Mrs. Adams, Sean's kindergarten teacher. "Maybe he'll outgrow it. Ritalin will help in the meantime."

Michael didn't buy it. "He's just a spirited kid," he said, indignant that Dr. Schaefer would prescribe Ritalin for his little boy. Other people's kids were hyperactive maybe, but not his. And Ritalin was screwy stuff. "It's a stimulant, yet the kids that take it act like zombies. Explain that." The suggestion of behavior modification under a psychologist's supervision was even worse. "The last thing that kid needs is a shrink. I don't want some psycho telling me how to raise my son."

Mona bought the Ritalin anyway and hid the bottle of white pills in her douche bag, where she knew Michael wouldn't find it. Today, she tells herself over and over again. Today I should have given it to him. But she can't bring herself to do it. That a stimulant could have a quieting effect doesn't phase her: Sean's behavior makes no sense, so why should the means to control it? But the possible side effects scare her, too. Plus, every article she's read says that Ritalin is over-prescribed.

Mona hears shuffling noises near the stairs. She rises and heads that way. She sent Sean to his room with crayons and a pad of paper half an hour ago, remembering how he spent hours drawing an orange cat eating a purple fish for Michael on Father's Day. "Sean," she calls from the stairs, picking up sheet after sheet of blank paper. No orange cats or purple fish, only a yellow elephant on the wall below the oak bannister and crayon wrappings all over the beige carpeting. "Sean!"

Sean rushes down the stairs and ducks past her. Mona grabs for him but misses. She almost runs him over in the foyer. "Don't color the walls," she says, grasping his arms and squeezing harder with each word, "color the paper."

"No." Sean spits the word at her. He pulls his arm away, blue eyes wet and wide.

"Go back to your room!" When Sean backs away from her, she grabs the back of his jeans and push-pulls him up the stairs.

She deposits a sobbing Sean in his room and returns to the kitchen wall, leaving the yellow elephant and crayon shavings for Michael. She scrubs till three fingernails break, scrubs till she hears Michael pull in the driveway. She quickly wipes down the wall and puts the sponge and cleanser under the sink.

After Michael settles into his leather recliner in the den, she sits on the arm of their tweed couch and picks at a ball of wool on her sweater. "Sean was really out of control today," she says finally.

"Well, control him." Michael flicks on the wide-screen TV and scans the channels.

"I think we should give him the Ritalin."

A bearded sportscaster starts talking about golf. Michael turns the volume up. "He knows you're a pushover, that's all. Can we talk about this later? I had a shitty day."

"Michael, I . . . ." The words won't come. "I threw a bowl of chili at your son today," she wants to say. But she knows what he'll say. "Grow up, Mona. Act your age."

Mona goes into the kitchen and checks the wall. Spotless. She pours a glass of chablis and thinks of her best friend, Janet, in Boston. A couple of months ago, she read an article about mothers who killed their children during fits of anger. She called Janet the next day. "Mothers like that should be put away," Mona said. "Can you believe anyone could do such a thing?" She told Janet about this beautiful little girl named Sarah who died from a blow to the head. But she didn't tell Janet about the dream. Sarah was asleep on Mona and Michael's king-sized waterbed. When Mona brought her milk and animal cookies, she awoke. She ate all of the milk and cookies, and Mona read to her from *Mother Goose*.

Mona sighs. She thinks of Sarah often, of having a little girl who will sit on her lap and let her do what mothers are supposed to do. Sean won't sit still long enough for her to read him a fairy tale. Yet there are precious moments. Swinging together on the wooden-seated swing at the cider mill, going higher and higher still, blue sky peeping through brown leaves like Sean's blue eyes through his long lashes. Riding the train to the city and spending hours in Fielding's toy department. Petting sheep, goats, and pigs at a local farm and picking a pumpkin to carve for Halloween.

Please help me remember the precious moments, Mona prays, climbing the stairs to check on Sean. She pauses at the top, struck by the stranger in the gold-plated oval mirror. Straight dark brown hair streaked with grey, blank brown eyes with half-moon shadows, pale skin with traces of adult acne.

She enters Sean's room and starts. The bed is empty. "Sean?" A shuffling sound answers. She glances toward the closet; the sound is closer. She walks around the bed, tripping on a cone-shaped pile of clothes and the dresser drawers they came from. A small hand shows through between the red bedspread and the floor. She reaches for the wrist.

"What are you doing?" she asks, jerking him to his feet. Sean stares at her with marble eyes. She studies his face: Michael's wavy blond hair and blue eyes, her mouth and nose. "I'm sorry, honey." Mona kneels to give him a hug. When she starts to rise, she sees a dark blue stain just below his elbow. She tries to wipe it off, gasping when she sees it's a bruise.

After dinner, Michael goes back into the den and Mona cleans up the kitchen. "Put those down," she tells Sean, who's found a pair of scissors and is making cutouts from the day's mail. He drops the scissors on the kitchen table and runs to Michael. "Not like that!" Mona gulps what's left of her wine. "Could you watch Sean while I walk the trail?"

"All right," Michael says, hoisting Sean onto his shoulders.

O

Mona follows the nature trail to where it forks, stopping behind the Fairfield Schools' satellite dish. The huge dish just doesn't belong in the grassy clearing. A wild-blackberry bush climbs the five-foot cyclone fence that surrounds the dish and adjacent tool shed. Mona kneels beside the fence and picks a handful of the dark berries. She squeezes them in her palm; purple-red juice oozes through their soft skin. She thinks about asking Dr. Schaefer about the support group he mentioned, even wonders what would happen if she took the Ritalin.

Mona walks the trail twice, till wet leaves cover her shoes and her feet feel the rocks beneath them. Arriving home just before dusk, she almost collides with Lindy Preston, who lives next door with three dogs and two cats. Mona says hi and gives Daisy, Lindy's buff-colored Cocker spaniel, a pat. "Make sure you hit my house on Halloween," Lindy says. Mona nods.

Sean talks about nothing but Halloween for the next three days. Mona spends every waking moment trying to keep him out of trouble. But when nighttime comes, she can't sleep: She thinks about Sarah, eats ice cream or leftovers, and sits in Michael's recliner and replays her bouts with Sean. She role-plays what she'll do and say the next time, practices counting to ten and being firm but loving.

She makes it through Devil's Night without losing her temper, and spends Halloween day working on Sean's devil's costume and setting up candy for Michael to pass out. After Michael gets home, she pulls the hood of Sean's red sweatshirt over his head, ties the drawstring, and smooths his red cotton cape. He pulls at her leg, determined to arrive at Lindy's before any of the other kids.

The air has a burnt-sugar smell that reminds her of past Halloweens, and she pauses, remembering trick-or-treating with her dad. Her mother made her costumes, but her father led her from house to house. He always knew which houses had the best candy, too. I wish he were here now, Mona thinks. He'd know how to handle Sean.

"Trick or treat! Trick or treat!" shout voices two or three houses away. Sean darts ahead of her. She catches up with him at Lindy's. "Don't do that again," she says, catching his right hand. "Now remember, just take one." Lindy comes to the door dressed like a martian and holds out a stainless steel bowl. "Two for you and one for Mom," she tells Sean, handing him three Mars bars.

"Let's go that way," Sean says, pointing toward the subdivision across the street.

"Let's do the lane first." Mona lets go of Sean's hand to button her cardigan, and he takes off, disappearing like a tail light down Winkler Lane.

"Sean!" Mona runs after him, stumbling over a pothole. As pain shoots up her left ankle, a figure darts across the road in front of her. She starts to follow but sees three larger children running to the door of Old Man Winkler's. A car pulls out of a driveway some twenty feet ahead of her. "Sean! Get back here!"

Her head pounds; her heart beats so fast it hurts. Doorbells ring up and down the lane; young voices cry "Trick or treat" in unison. Mona sees a flash of red through the trees and runs that way. Little Red Riding Hood with her mother. She passes more red on the left. A mailbox. More red on the right. A red sumac. Sean steps from behind the sumac. "That's it." She grabs the hood of his sweatshirt and drags him up the lane. She slows down when he whines "You're hurting me," but she doesn't stop.

When they reach Lindy's house, she pauses. She kneels down and looks Sean in the face, an innocent face any mother would love. She reties his hood's drawstring with shaky fingers. "Let's try the Johnson's," she says with effort, forcing herself to put her arm around his shoulders.

Later that evening, Michael helps Sean sort through his loot. Sean gives Michael the hard candy to take on his Chicago trip. Mona wishes they were both going. I wish we could talk things out, she thinks. But we won't talk—not Michael and I, not Sean and I. We'll keep our masks on, pretending everything's okay.

○

The next morning, Michael leaves for the Artificial Intelligence conference in Chicago. Mona walks Sean to school. Back home, she doesn't know what to do first. She fusses with her hair: curls it, puts it in a ponytail, tucks one side behind an ear and brushes the other side forward. She gives up, deciding to read instead. She sits down in Michael's recliner and picks up *People*. The article about Princess Caroline's husband dying in a powerboat accident and leaving three small children fatherless makes her cry. She puts the magazine down. She wants a glass of wine but decides to nap instead.

Mona sinks into the king-sized waterbed and closes her eyes. She lets go of her arms and legs, head and neck, like the relaxation tapes instruct. She thinks of Sarah, with the wheat curls and sky eyes. Sean's eyes. She imagines dressing Sarah in a lace-trimmed white dress and giving her Sean's teddy bear.

The slam of a door breaks the silence. Mona opens her eyes. Michael should be in Chicago; she's not supposed to get Sean till one. She hears footsteps in the kitchen, on the stairs. A burglar? She jumps up.

"Mommy, where are you? Mrs. Adams made me lay down after snack. I hate it. I'm never going back."

Mona grabs Sean's shoulders. "How'd you get home?" she asks, shaking him.

"Mommmeeee, don't," Sean cries.

"Mommmeeee, don't," she mimics, pushing him into his room and slamming the door. She leans against the wall, shivery. "I'm sorry," she tells Sean through the closed door. She wants to hold him, to tell him she's sorry, but she's afraid to go into his room. She hears Sean crying and starts to cry, too.

Michael calls just after five. "There's nothing to cry about," he says when Mona tearfully explains what happened. "I'll be home tomorrow afternoon. We'll take Sean to Mom's and go out for dinner and talk everything out. I promise."

Mona puts Sean to bed at eight. She reads *People* till her eyelids flutter. Sarah comes to her just before daybreak, wearing the lace-trimmed dress and carrying Sean's teddy bear. Motioning for Mona to follow, she flies out the bedroom window and heads toward Fairfield Schools' satellite dish. A blue halo surrounds the dish, illuminating the tool shed and the clearing below. Sarah takes Mona's hand and helps her land. She leads her to the tool shed door, which is ajar, and then disappears. A burlap bag lays in the middle of the shed floor. Mona inches toward it.

She awakes with a start, trembling. She's slept through the alarm clock but somehow manages to get Sean dressed and to kindergarten. The phone rings at ten. Fingers greasy from buttering cold toast, she waits for the answering machine's click.

"Honey, I'm going to have to stay over one more night," Michael says. "If you're home, pick up the phone."

She grabs the phone. "You promised."

"Honey, hang on." Mona hangs up and takes the receiver off the hook.

At one p.m., she picks up Sean.

"Mona," Mrs. Adams says, "Do you have a minute?"

"Yes."

"Sean was upset again today. He didn't want to eat his snack, and when I tried to get him to take his nap, he ran out of the room."

"I'm sorry, Mrs. Adams. He's hyper sometimes, that's all."

"Are there problems at home? He seems agitated."

"Maybe he's not ready for this. I'm sorry, but I've got to go. My husband's due home soon."

Sean runs to the refrigerator the minute they walk in the door. "I'm hungry," he says, pulling out the container of leftover chili. He has his fingers in the cold chili before Mona can take it away from him.

"Let me warm it," Mona says, grabbing the chili and giving him a handful of oyster crackers instead. "Go sit in the den for a minute."

"I'm sorry for losing my temper yesterday, Sean," she continues, dishing the chili and putting it in the microwave. The bowl burns her hands when she gets it out. She wraps a towel around it and heads for the den. She finds cracker crumbs on the glass-topped coffee table, but no Sean. She climbs the stairs, sees Sean running in mindless circles in his room, and goes into her bedroom. She puts the chili on the vanity and closes her eyes. Black spots move back and forth before them, then white spots. White spots with numbers on them.

Mona gets her douche bag out of the vanity and reaches for the Ritalin. She carefully removes one of the white pills and crushes it into crumb-sized bits. "Your chili's ready," she says loudly enough for Sean to hear, stirring the powdery white crumbs into the bowl of chili and watching them disappear.

Resting Places

When the Boy Scout jackknife my brother Dan left me fell through the grate, I panicked. I kicked the grate till my foot throbbed, hoping to jar it loose. When that didn't work, I tried to pry it open with my hands. Grease and blood dirtied my fingernails, and I sank onto the cement floor and whimpered. I was alone in the garage, the garage where my father and his father before him had tinkered with tractors and trucks, the garage where Dan had attached a hose to the exhaust, carefully closed three doors—to the kitchen, the garage, and his red Miata—and cranked the engine.

I'd carried his jackknife in my purse since the funeral, losing it twice. The second time, I'd given a $100 reward for the purse's return, but it was the jackknife I wanted. I sat on the cold cement and thought hard about what to do: call a handyman or plumber to fish it out, find a crowbar of sorts and try again myself, or wait and see if my father had a better idea.

From the cement floor, I could just see the olive-green canvas bags that held matching Remington 30-06 rifles. My father still polished them three times yearly, although it had been two years since he and Dan had used them. "Beauties," Dan had called them, "bolt-action beauties." Seductive but not beautiful, I thought, reluctantly rising and walking their way. I partially unzipped one bag and touched the rifle's silky barrel. Then I flinched, imagining the barrel hot in my hand. I couldn't stand hunting, but hunting was why I was here. Dramatic irony, I supposed: When I was little, I used to beg my father to take me hunting. He took Dan instead.

The garage door swung open, catching me off guard.

"Oh, it's you," my father said, balancing himself on two canes, not the canes the drugstore sells, but hand-crafted ones with deer-antler handles. A walker was what my father's rheumatoid arthritis called for, but he couldn't part with those canes. "Your mother and I went for last-minute supplies. You ready?"

"I'm ready."

He grunted. "This wasn't my idea."

"I brought some books along—I won't get in the way."

"Your mother's full of crazy ideas these days."

Mother overheard him from some six feet behind. "Crazy?

59

Crazy is getting a permit to hunt deer from a car and going up north with that car to keep you company."

"Without Dan to keep you company" is what she meant, of course. "I like the woods, Dad," I said. "I really do." This was no lie: I liked to walk in the woods, to hear leaves brush each other's cheeks, to see laser beams of light pierce the undergrowth. But this would be no walk in the woods; it would be deer-hunting detail. I owed it to him, though. I owed it to Dan.

Mother handed me the grocery bag she'd been carrying: hunter's sausage, a six-pack of apple juice, peanuts, bananas, and raisins. "I know you do, Brenda." She looked at me strangely. "What happened to your hands?"

"I locked myself out of my car," I lied, deciding to let the jackknife rest. "You have no idea how hard it is to break into a car nowadays." As soon as the words were out, I hated my mouth. Mother knew just how hard it was, having attacked the Miata's driver's side window with a coathanger. Father had smashed the window instead, sending shatterproof glass everywhere.

O

I parked the Mercury Marquis off a hunting trail between McVety Road and Butterfield Creek and opened a can of apple juice. "Want one?" I asked my father, who was staring at the stand of trees as if he'd never seen a tree before.

"Nature calls," he said a moment later, opening up the car door and pulling himself up by the door handle.

I shook my head as he picked his way toward a grandfather oak, wondering what I'd do when I couldn't hold it any longer. I couldn't just leave my father in these woods, yet I couldn't ask him to come with me to the motor lodge restroom every hour or so. Prevention is best, I decided, opening the driver's door and dumping the apple juice.

My father returned after a few minutes, and the wait began.

"Is your book any good?" he asked an hour later.

"Good enough."

"At least you didn't bring *The Deerslayer*," he said.

"You mean *The Deer Hunter*."

"No, *The Deerslayer*. By James Fenimore Cooper."

"Never read it."

"Me, either," he said.

We laughed awkwardly. It wasn't even that funny, but we needed that laugh.

The first doe appeared two-and-a-half hours later out of nowhere, a wood sprite with black-fringed eyes and a brown velvet coat. I sucked in my breath. I knew my father wouldn't shoot a doe. As luck would have it, a buck was right behind her, followed by another doe and a white-speckled fawn.

They gathered in the clearing just beyond us and began grazing. My father stood, raised his rifle shoulder high, and took a half-step their way. The fawn and the first doe continued grazing, but the second doe and the buck heard the alarm in the crackling leaves. They both spun east, but the buck tilted his head our way. We were close enough to see his nose twitch and his eyes blink, close enough to sense distrust in his blood.

I knew enough about hunting from listening to my father and Dan to look at his rack, and I knew enough about racks to count his antlers. An eight-point—not a big buck but respectable enough. I gave my father a sideways glance. His rifle was still in place, but he'd made no move to shoot. I felt that jittery feeling that too much caffeine and sugar bring on, although I'd had neither, and had this insane urge to jump around or run, anything to break the picture before me.

My father raised his rifle into the air. Before he could shoot, I let my book slip through my fingers. It made a soft thud, just loud enough to spook the deer. They bounded north and then veered west, white tails waving good riddance.

"Oops," I said, wrapping my arm around my father's.

"What the hell did you do that for?" he asked.

I patted his arm. "It slipped. I'm sorry . . . it just slipped."

"Forget it," my father said, drawing his arm away. "He wasn't worth the effort."

I almost questioned this—an eight-point was an eight-point, right?—but didn't.

We settled back in the Marquis and broke into the hunter's sausage. It was tough and stringy, kind of like my father. Dan, I decided, had been prime rib—rare and tender, cut in the prime of life.

"Tired, Brenda?" my father asked after we'd picked through the peanuts, bananas, and raisins. We'd seen no more deer, and I doubted there were more to see. We were relatively near McVety Road, one deterrent, and that earlier shot should have frightened away other deer, too.

"Not really," I said, thinking I'd humor him. We had quite a night ahead of us—dinner at Dagwood's Place, where my father and Dan always ate, followed by a night at the motor lodge, where my father and Dan never stayed. They'd always camped, the one thing I refused to do.

"Good. Maybe I'll get that buck yet."

We waited. And when it seemed we'd waited enough . . . that we could guiltlessly call it a day . . . my father raised his left index finger, a sign I remembered well from childhood. One solitary buck stood about twenty-five yards behind us; one solitary twelve-point buck. One solitary twelve-point buck who was worth the effort. Prime rib. Not aged; not tough and stringy. He'll kill it, I thought. He'll kill it and say it's for Dan.

My father eased the car door open, twisted around in his seat, and aimed the rifle. Despite my prayers, the buck didn't move. I closed my eyes, bracing for the shot and the pandemonium that would follow.

I jumped when the shot rang out. When I opened my eyes, though, the buck wasn't lying dead or wounded on the ground, and my father wasn't inching his way toward him one painful cane step at a time. No, my father was slumped in the passenger seat of his Marquis, eyes hooded, a weary half-smile on his face.

"Missed," he said.

"You missed?"

"You try shooting from the car."

"I would have thought shooting from the car would be easier. I mean, you are sitting down . . . "

"It's not working," he snapped. "It doesn't feel right."

"Maybe tomorrow . . . "

"Not tomorrow. I told you, it doesn't feel right."

As I started the car, I tried to recall if my father had ever actually gotten a deer. He and Dan had brought home a ten-point a few years back, but I couldn't honestly say who'd claimed it. Most probably Dan. He'd loved the chase; he'd loved the raw power of the Remington 30-06 in his hands and the way it gleamed when struck by sun. And he'd loved the beauty of any well-executed act. There was a blessing in that: Dan could have turned the Remington on himself but had chosen a more civilized way. To my father, though, the execution didn't matter. To him, I decided, the kill had become as incomprehensible as Dan's final act. As incomprehensible as me trying to replace him.

I didn't put any of this into words; that would have killed the understanding. But after we pulled onto McVety Road and passed Butterfield Creek—on that stretch that's so bumpy you can't go over ten mph—my father turned his head. I saw him look back, look back and imagine that twelve-point buck he'd let go stopping and drinking deeply from the creek. I saw him lower his head. I saw him lift it up.

Photo by Rick Smith.

Nancy Ryan's work appears in *The Creative Writer's Craft* (National Textbook Company, 1998), *The Reality of Breastfeeding* (Greenwood Publishing Group, 1998), *Variations on the Ordinary: A Woman's Reader* (Plain View Press, 1995), and *Getting the Knack* (National Council of Teachers of English, 1992). Ryan is also co-author of the children's play *Buttonbush* (Player's Press, 1996) and three books of nonfiction. She received honors in both the 1997 Detroit Women Writers' Drama Competition and the 1996 DWW Short Story Competition.

Miriam Moore, cover artist, paints watercolors and makes artist books in San Antonio, where she is raising two delightful daughters. She has a Bachelor of Arts degree from the University of Texas at San Antonio.